MODERN
RUSTIC

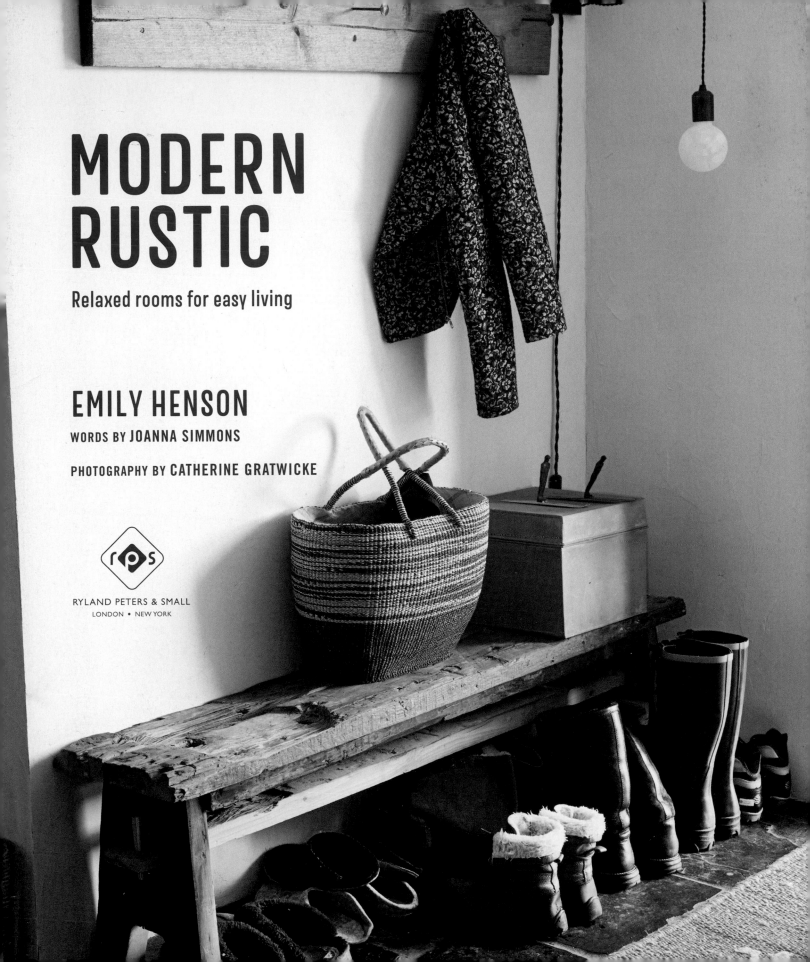

MODERN RUSTIC

Relaxed rooms for easy living

EMILY HENSON

WORDS BY JOANNA SIMMONS

PHOTOGRAPHY BY CATHERINE GRATWICKE

RYLAND PETERS & SMALL
LONDON • NEW YORK

DESIGNER Megan Smith
EDITOR Rebecca Woods
LOCATION RESEARCH Emily Henson
    and Jess Walton
HEAD OF PRODUCTION Patricia Harrington
ART DIRECTOR Leslie Harrington
EDITORIAL DIRECTOR Julia Charles

STYLING Emily Henson
INDEXER Diana LeCore

First published in 2013
This edition published in 2021
by Ryland Peters & Small
20–21 Jockey's Fields
London WC1R 4BW

and
341 E 116th St
New York, NY 10029
www.rylandpeters.com

Text copyright © Emily Henson
    2013, 2021
Design and photographs
    copyright © Ryland Peters
    & Small 2013, 2021

10 9 8 7 6 5 4 3 2 1

ISBN 978-1-78879-186-1

A CIP record for this book is available
from the British Library.

Library of Congress CIP data has been
applied for.

Printed and bound in China

CONTENTS

INTRODUCTION

Paint shades, wallpapers, fabrics and finishes – the modern home can be decked out and dressed in every colour and pattern under the sun. But in recent years, an earthy, gutsy interiors trend has emerged as the perfect antidote to this embarrassment of decorating riches – modern rustic. In it, interiors are laid elegantly bare, with striking details such as soaring rafters or exposed stone walls taking centre stage. The beautiful bones of a property are

ABOVE LEFT & RIGHT Rustic wooden beams, pillars and lintels support this renovated Dutch farm building and contrast with modern touches like the sleek concrete floors. Walls are plastered with a stucco made using local river clay, which has been softly coloured using natural pigments. The result is a rustic wall treatment that is both environmentally friendly and offers excellent soundproofing, too.

celebrated, as are materials, furniture and textiles that have sprung straight from the natural world, bursting with organic beauty.

Modern rustic style suits our current mood. In these austere times, we want our homes to look authentic, not flashy; we want our rooms to feel grounded and safe, not self-conscious and styled. In the modern rustic home, muted colours, natural materials, sensual textures and a love of simple, skilfully designed furniture creates spaces with real warmth

and integrity. Every piece must earn its place in a modern rustic scheme, from the sofa to the saucepans, but the overall feel is relaxed, enveloping and calm. Despite its use of recycled materials and objects, this is not a typical vintage look; it is more original than that. Modern rustic incorporates the latest interior design know-how and exciting, contemporary materials, and brings rusticity with all its honest, unpretentious appeal, beautifully up to date.

ABOVE LEFT A combination of reclaimed woods, with different tones and finishes, has been used to make the door, walls and even the exterior porch area in this striking Californian home.
ABOVE RIGHT Walls panelled in simple, untreated wood create a rustic backdrop for lush textures, homely furniture and decorations taken straight from nature in this welcoming Norwegian mountain cabin.

Modern Rustic features inspiring homes around the world, from ranch houses in Los Angeles to Norwegian cabins, to illustrate this brilliantly back-to-basics style. It shows how any place, from a compact cottage to a featureless modern apartment, can gain gritty personality when peppered with rustic notes. It is a look that urges us to ditch the paint charts, put away those wallpaper swatches and welcome the natural world inside – with soothing, sumptuous results.

INSPIRATIONS

Pure rustic style, as its name suggests, is all about interiors pared back to the bare essentials. The raw materials of a home, from its ceiling rafters to its wooden floorboards, are the star attractions, and bright colours or fussy fabrics are a no–no! Instead, brick walls and stone stairs bring rough texture to an interior, while warm wood in every finish, from silky smooth to weather-beaten, creates an atmosphere of profound calm. Pure rustic is primal and soothing, but versatile, too – don't imagine that this strand of modern rustic style only works in a craggy Scottish croft or low-ceilinged cottage. In fact, it effortlessly brings character to any blank-canvas home, whether that is an architect-designed house or a featureless flat, giving it depth, soul and masses of earthy appeal.

PURE RUSTIC

ABOVE LEFT Patterns and bright colours do not suit a pure rustic scheme, but plain china in clean shades, here arranged on a slab of wood, looks perfect.
LEFT A simple bench against an unadorned wall creates an eye-catching and beautiful pause point in this pure rustic home.

ABOVE RIGHT A length of rope running alongside these stairs makes a rustic and original alternative to a wooden handrail. A versatile contemporary material, concrete has been used for flooring throughout this space. It is polished to create a smooth, softly reflective surface.

OPPOSITE A huge sliding panel, similar to those found on film sets, allows the open-plan space in this home to be divided, to create a cosy living area separate from the larger cooking, dining and work spaces. It has been painted with lime paint, which creates a chalky, nuanced finish.

OPPOSITE A palette of greys has been used throughout this renovated Dutch home, creating a calm, grown-up atmosphere. The heavy oak table and stool are balanced by chairs upholstered in soft fabric, while the chandeliers add some sparkle and glamour. The portrait is by artist Christiaan Lieverse.

THIS PAGE In this renovated period house, modern touches such as the polished concrete staircase are introduced in combination with traditional materials, such as soft lime paint. A chandelier keeps the look the luxe side of rustic.

Pure rustic style is the most elegant and simple of all the modern rustic looks. Just as a chef can create a beautiful dish from a few quality ingredients, so the most striking pure rustic homes rely on a handful of gorgeous materials for their unique character. Whether these materials form part of the structure or are the toothsome seasoning to an all-white scheme, they will help to create a space brimming with beauty and integrity.

Some houses are packed with original features – stone walls, wooden floorboards,

ABOVE LEFT & RIGHT, & OPPOSITE This striking Norwegian home boasts plenty of rustic materials, from woods to brick and sheepskin, but has used each in original ways. The floors, for example, are polished concrete with thin strips of wood interspersed, while the walls above the fireplace are lined with fibre cement board, typically used as exterior cladding.

chunky roof beams – and these details, however small, should be allowed to stand out. Consider exposing architectural features, too. Plaster can be chiselled from a brick fire surround or a ceiling removed to reveal a soaring roof. Alternatively, add the handsome materials yourself. Clad walls in timber and, for a cohesive but textured look, choose different woods and various finishes, whether that is untreated, painted or sealed and smooth.

Pure rustic style also works brilliantly in a neutral space. It will warm up stark modern

LEFT The ground floor of this Scottish house dates from the 17th century, with a first floor built in 1809 and a modern extension recently added at the back. The owners incorporated original features like these stone steps, which were originally on the exterior, and used reclaimed materials throughout.

boards or chunky earthenware vessels on the work surface. Similarly, a smart modern tap/faucet and contemporary trough sink can be mounted on a slab of reclaimed timber, for a happy marriage of old and new.

Choose furniture from across the decades. Vintage items, passed down from granny or sourced at markets, are a good fit, as are used objects with an industrial edge – think anglepoise lights or workbench stools. You can even venture onto the high street for inspiration. Modern sofas with clean lines and the odd cool, contemporary piece in an unlikely material such as Perspex will fit in. Seek out today's craftsmen, too, who use wood to create examples of classic furniture that are both solid and timeless.

architecture or create personality in featureless rooms. This can be achieved by weaving exciting natural materials into the fabric of each room, but for a faster fix, simply look to furniture, textiles and paint finishes to supply the rustic wow factor. Plain white walls are a clean backdrop to rustic furniture, while deep, natural colours such as grey, sage and stormy blue will add drama. Choose chalky, matt finishes or explore the world of organic, textured paints. Natural lime paint, for instance, creates a pleasingly uneven finish and comes in subtle, natural tones.

Pure rustic style is adept at blending modern and rustic, so if your tastes range naturally towards the clean and sleek, you can satisfy them here! Install a row of new, white kitchen units, then warm them up by displaying chopping

OPPOSITE The cupboards in the dining space of this Scottish home have a solid feel, echoing the rocks on which the house sits. They are made with oak from old French railway carriages/railroad cars.

RIGHT A modern extension on a centuries-old Scottish property is bursting with rustic touches, including a large island unit made from reclaimed wood and pine flooring salvaged from a London warehouse.

The scale and quantity of furniture is as important as its provenance. A few larger items, such as a rustic refectory table or beautiful leather sofa, will keep the look cool, not cluttered. Many of the other pieces we typically fill our homes with do not suit the pure rustic look, so think carefully about what you really need. Consider building in discreet storage, where clutter can be hidden, allowing those items of furniture that make the cut to be fully appreciated.

The colours of a pure rustic scheme come predominantly from the materials and furniture within it. Whites, greys and woody tones dominate, but any colour that seems to have leapt straight from nature's palette will blend in or provide a gentle accent. A single chair upholstered in mossy green, for example, makes a stylish focal point in a cool grey scheme. Add fresh flowers, too, for little pops of organic colour and sprinkle in a few mirrors and glass pieces, from jars to candlesticks, to help bounce light around and add sparkle to this elegant look.

RIGHT Perched on a hill in Los Angeles, this beautiful home boasts long views over the valley. Two chairs with reindeer hide-seats by Icelandic designer Sveinn Kjarval and a clutch of rustic tables fashioned from tree trunks create a little seating area by the huge windows. A soft rug layered with an animal hide adds a further rustic splash and prevents this bright, modern space from feeling stark.

All modern rustic schemes glory in teaming the rough with the smooth, but bohemian rustic blends in a little colour, pattern and detail, too. That rustic staple, wood, still features, but it is matched with pale white walls or even painted brickwork, for a fresh contrast. Bold statements such as a wall clad in dark reclaimed wood create plenty of gritty drama, while bohemian elements, from textiles to trinkets, add pockets of intriguing detail and gentle humour. Junk-shop furniture brings some pre-loved character to each space and there is delicious pattern and colour to enjoy in the form of folksy, embroidered fabrics, vintage wallpaper and quirky, decorative objects. The result is a rustic look that is organic, cosy and welcoming.

BOHEMIAN RUSTIC

ABOVE LEFT The wooden handles on this cutlery/flatware teamed with vintage china patterned with gold creates a beautiful marriage of the decorative and the rustic.

LEFT Old wooden and cane birdcages suspended next to a colourful, quirky ceiling light are a creative and attractive alternative to traditional lampshades.

ABOVE RIGHT A battered metal container makes a pleasingly rustic home for a bunch of colourful ranunculus flowers.

OPPOSITE This house, built in the 1960s, was stripped of its reproduction coving and carpet by its owners, who then clad walls in reclaimed larch, to bring the natural world inside. The wood came from trees blown down in Kew Gardens during the hurricane of 1987. The sideboard was bought for £20, stripped back and personalized with patterned wallpaper.

Scouring second-hand fairs or junk shops for unusual vintage finds or upcycling old, time-worn objects is an interiors trend that is still going strong, and this impulse to reuse and recycle also drives the bohemian rustic look. Buying and restoring a one-off object satisfies our wallet as well as our conscience, since it is both economical and green. Bohemian rustic celebrates this win-win situation and goes one better, finding exciting new roles for vintage pieces and exploring bold ways to use reclaimed raw materials in the domestic landscape.

ABOVE & OPPOSITE In this colourful den, a gorgeous feature has been created by papering the inside of old drawers and mounting them on the wall. Surprising and creative, these decorative drawers add both a rustic note and a splash of colour and pattern to a plain background. They are also the perfect display space for quirky finds and favourite objects,

including little bird and animal figures, perched on miniature chairs. Inexpensive to make, this wall art is eco-friendly, too, relying on salvaged furniture finds and scraps of wallpaper. Similarly, old pieces of fabric were used to make the cushion covers. Teamed with a sheepskin throw, these cushions now perfectly soften a retro cane hanging chair.

When the owners of this Dutch home began renovation work on it, they wanted to give what was then a collection of old barns and store houses a very modern rethink. They preserved original features such as the dramatic beams and quaint arched windows (which now have new frames), but added zesty colours, concrete flooring and modern innovations such as underfloor heating. The idea was to give an ancient building a second chance as a whole new style of property, while sidestepping any traditional country-house restoration clichés. Now, bold pops of colour on soft furnishings and artwork give the muted, rustic backdrop life and humour.

Wood, once again, is central to this look, but teaming different types and finishes gives bohemian rustic spaces their energy. In a single room, you might find white glossed floorboards, distressed wooden cladding and sexy black tongue-and-groove panelling – and that's just the surfaces! When teamed with chunky furniture, from a painted chair to a knotty table, a layered, relaxed look begins to emerge.

Modern materials also take their place alongside this abundance of timber. A hard composite work surface, a polished concrete sink, a contemporary tap/faucet – these ensure the look stays exciting. They are also the kind of high-performance, professional ingredients that improve the ergonomics and longevity of hard-working spaces such as the bathroom and kitchen. To ensure these modern elements do not jar with the rustic backdrop, choose neutral shades and organic finishes – a worktop the colour of stone is preferable to a white, seamless Corian design, for example. Think neutral and unflashy and you cannot go wrong.

When it comes to furniture, second-hand finds give a bohemian rustic space real personality. A grand, striking

piece that has 'unique' written all over it will become a focal point in any room, while smaller, utilitarian items such as sideboards and plan chests combine storage with vintage good looks. There are no rules about what fits in, so experiment with different combinations of furniture, from various periods, and always keep your eyes peeled for exciting gems.

Look for ways to personalize second-hand pieces, too. Could you add new drawer handles or pretty glass knobs, or line shelves with vintage wallpaper? Always think out of the box and consider how your second-hand finds could be also be repurposed. An old birdcage or lobster pot can become a dramatic lampshade, for example, while a wooden drawer mounted on the wall becomes an artwork and space for display combined. Finally, consider restoring or even building furniture. Painted wooden furniture can be stripped and sealed, while rustic raw materials such as timber planks can be used to make a simple shelf, table or bedhead.

Although many rustic schemes rely on materials for depth and interest, bohemian rustic rooms also embrace colour and pattern. Of course, that does not mean chucking chintz around your carefully crafted rustic space! Instead, choose ethnic or folksy patterns in rich reds, greens and pinks, for a fresh contrast to a raw, unfinished backdrop. Work in some texture with your colour and pattern, too. Fabrics that are traditional or ethnic, whether that is Indian crewelwork or vintage velour, have great tactile appeal.

Clutter is not welcome in any rustic scheme, but artfully displayed pieces, from pictures to jewellery, lend a bohemian rustic room a softer, more personal feel. This love of simple, informal display sets the bohemian look apart from some of its more muscular rustic relatives, and creates small corners of detail. Look at the things you already own, then think creatively about how to display them. Hang beads from a row of hooks, drape fairy lights from antlers or put up antique picture frames to make a low-key artwork.

ABOVE LEFT & TOP LEFT A ceramic tealight holder and recycled glass tumblers add pools of shine and brightness to their respective wooden table tops, which are beautifully rustic and raw.

ABOVE A chunky trestle table and wooden chairs softened by animal skins form the perfect dining space in this rustic Norwegian cabin. The steel pendant is a shiny contrast to the wood.

OPPOSITE Wood-clad walls tend to absorb light, but this effect is offset here by white-painted floorboards, which help bounce around the natural light that pours in through the large windows.

Highly original and super fun, the pop rustic look is light, bright and easy to live with. It blasts a gale of fresh air through traditional rustic style, and while it shares a love of materials and natural finishes with all the rustic looks seen so far, it combines this with clean lines, design-classic furniture and shots of deliciously bright orange, yellow and pink. Instead of raw, unfinished timber, pale plywood and wood veneers feature on walls and flooring.

Exposed brickwork is punctuated with graphic art or hip posters and wooden boards are brightened with eye-catching rugs boasting geometric prints and stripes. Weave in a few funky, ultra-modern fixtures, such as oversized lights in plastic and metal, and you have a look that is sunny, not serious; happy, not heavy.

POP RUSTIC

ABOVE LEFT Incorporating brilliant colours and contemporary materials such as plastic gives a pop rustic scheme its energy.
LEFT Wood plays a huge role in this kitchen, but its honey tones are punctuated by the vibrant orange legs of these stools.

ABOVE RIGHT A contemporary chair in a zingy yellow makes a striking contrast to the planting, concrete and wood in this outdoor space.
OPPOSITE Wooden panelling is a staple of modern rustic homes, but here smooth planks have been chosen, for a sleeker, lighter look.

The timber is hung horizontally, which helps the space feel wider, and then contrasted with a custom-made sofa, covered with vintage aeroplane seating fabric, and a stainless-steel table. The painting, just seen, is by Aaron Morse.

Pop rustic is a confident, energized look. Taking basic materials and using them in a non-traditional way demands a certain design chutzpah, after all, but that is exactly what the pop rustic look does so well. Plywood, concrete, timber and tiles are teamed with fresh colours or cast in unusual roles to create exciting interiors. Materials that would not be included in many rustic schemes are welcomed here, from plastic to painted metal and shiny chrome. Furniture with clean lines balances all this exuberance and keeps the look uncluttered, while bursts of colour and pattern further boost the light, bright mood.

Wood again features in a pop rustic home, but it is used rather differently. It still crops up widely, not simply as flooring but as something to clad walls or kitchen islands in, or to construct partitions and built-in storage from. Instead of the dark or rough woods used in many modern rustic homes, however, woods that are beautifully smooth and radiantly pale are the stars here. Large stretches of skinny, honey-toned flooring create an expansive, airy

RIGHT This home combines rustic touches, including a brick wall and wooden panelling, with a contemporary configuration. A pantry is hidden inside the ply clad 'room' in the centre, with a painting by Peter Klara hanging against it, and splashes of colour lead the eye around the space. The pink on the sofa is picked up on the dining table, while pops of orange and yellow add vibrancy in the kitchen.

feel, while walls faced with a pale wood veneer are teamed with white plaster for a fresh rustic feel that is never overpowering.

Wooden furniture is another key ingredient, but its lines are clean and crisp. Look for modern versions of classic staples such as an oblong dining table and benches, choosing pieces that are solid but sleek. Furniture that combines wood with other materials keeps the look light, too. Stools with wooden seats and painted metal legs, for example, or a wooden-framed sofa topped with jewel-bright upholstery inject exciting contrast into a pop rustic scheme.

If your wallet permits, splash out on elegant mid-century pieces, too. Furniture designers of the 1950s, such as Charles and Ray Eames, Norman Cherner, Hans Wegner and Arne Jacobsen, used exciting materials and techniques to create pieces with a light, natural appearance. Moulded veneered plywood, leather and even woven paper cord all feature on classic designs of this period and perfectly suit a pop rustic scheme, bringing welcome elegance and character. Look out for painted wooden furniture, or get your paintbrush out and create your own. A single stool picked out in a hot, acid shade creates a witty accent, while chairs painted matt black or dark grey are a good foil to a space already bursting with woody tones.

A love of colour sets the pop rustic look apart from other modern rustic schemes.

OPPOSITE Wooden flooring, cabinetry and cladding bring warmth to this space, but some walls are simply painted white and others only partially clad to keep the look crisp. Against this, classic chairs by Norman Cherner look chic and elegant.

THIS PAGE A concrete shelf against a white wall is the perfect place to display favourite objects. Installing it low down also accentuates the ceiling height, as the eye moves up from the display to the soaring vertical space above.

RIGHT & FAR RIGHT Even the tiniest touches of colour can brighten a rustic scheme, and when used minimally, neon shades work well. Here, a string of orange stars and the pink wool tied to a teaspoon sing out.
BELOW There is a folksy-meets-funky edge to this dining space, thanks to the orange lampshade, moulded plastic seating and ply walls. The colourful artwork is City of Elephants by Geoff McFetridge.
OPPOSITE Surprising combinations of materials and colours give this kitchen its unique feel. Wooden beams, a paving-style floor and painted brickwork are clashed with pops of neon on china, painted by the owner.

Colour is used frequently, and not simply sludgy neutrals but bright, neon shades. This is a huge departure from the natural tones beloved by most modern rustic homes, yet these colours create an energy and sense of fun that is hugely enjoyable to live with. Rather than splashing pink paint up the walls, though, colours are introduced on furniture, upholstery, rugs and artwork. They are accents only, and will not fight with the rustic backdrop of wood, brick or simple white paint.

Pomegranate pink, retro orange and lemon yellow crop up time and again and, in addition to adding some zing, they can be cleverly used to lead the eye around an open-plan space. The pink on a sofa may be picked up on the legs of the dining chairs and then found again on china in the kitchen. Where possible, colour and function combine, too, so that this look remains grounded. An iron cooking pot in hot orange, for example, or a table with a pink top are both useful and beautiful, adding dots of colour.

Fearless, sexy and complex, the retro rustic look is influenced by the architecture and design of the 1950s and 1970s, but works in plenty of modern, innovative magic to bring the best elements from those decades up to date. This is a grown-up style of modern rustic, where heavyweight materials, from steel and breeze/cinder blocks, to wood and concrete, sit side by side, filling each room with brooding good looks and rich colour. More is definitely more in a retro rustic home, too, and this intense backdrop is bravely embellished with striking displays and unique objects. Vintage artwork, animal skins, coloured ceramics and lots of plants all add to the lush, decadent atmosphere, producing a home with depth, dignity and detail.

RETRO RUSTIC

ABOVE LEFT Glass and mirrors beautifully brighten dark wood. Here, a vintage mirror stands out against wooden panelling and creates a bright focal point.

LEFT An assortment of books stacked horizontally on a built-in sideboard.

ABOVE RIGHT A collection of small artworks and curios is proudly displayed on this built-in shelving, including, intriguingly, a huge potato carved from wood!

OPPOSITE The raw materials and original features are preserved and celebrated in this Californian house, designed by architect A. Quincy Jones, who was based in Los Angeles during the 1950s and 1960s. Breeze/cinder block walls, concrete floors and wood-panelled ceilings create a dark, earthy atmosphere that the owner's furniture does not attempt to water down. This gleaming black leather armchair, for example, is as austere and bold as its surroundings.

A good way to understand the retro rustic look is to picture the simple, modernist residences, originally pioneered by architect Cliff May, that were the post-war dream home for middle-class Americans. Known as California Ranch Houses, these suburban dwellings incorporated modernist ideas and styles – such as minimal use of interior decoration and a single-storey layout – to create an informal, casual living style.

Retro rustic borrows some of the spirit and styling of the ranch house, such as exposed roof beams and stone fireplaces, but clashes and layers materials for a funky, contemporary update. Wood featured then, as it features now, but a retro rustic home uses a mix of timbers to create visual and tactile variety. Darker woods are favoured and their toffee and conker-brown tones give a space a grown-up, sexy vibe. Wood appears on ceilings, wall panelling, floors, built-in furniture – you name it – but to keep the overall appearance stimulating, it is contrasted with other surfaces, such as stainless steel in

ABOVE & OPPOSITE
Displayed against the masculine bones of this Californian home, designed by architect A. Quincy Jones, are the owner's unique and interesting pieces. There is space to relax, too, with sofas arranged by the fire and a day bed overlooking the inviting living space.

a kitchen, or installed in eye-catching ways: think slim floorboards laid on the diagonal, for example.

This is a masculine style, where drama, ergonomics and the integrity of the building are paramount. The house's architectural features are celebrated – the more gritty they are, the better! Breeze/cinder-block walls would look spare and cold in most homes, but when teamed with warm wood, lend heft and style to a retro rustic space. They may be combined with other gutsy materials such as brick or polished concrete, creating a look that is defiantly bold.

The furniture in a retro rustic home must hold its own against the dramatic bones of each room. Vintage pieces are a safe bet, combining timeless style with a rich patina that suits this materials-conscious look. Glossy leather upholstery, bent wood chairs and neat sofas and day beds all feel at home. These can be scattered with patterned cushions, or softened with a knitted throw. At floor level, knock some of the hard edges off austere furniture by combining it with decadent furs, patterned rugs or mats woven from natural sisal or coir.

Built-in storage is a classic period ingredient that still works wonderfully today. From shelves that act as partitions

OPPOSITE Rustic stone, exposed brick and wooden ceiling panels – this LA home has the retro rustic look sewn up. Cream carpet softens these raw materials, while plants and artworks personalize the gritty backdrop.

ABOVE LEFT A pleasing pattern of shelves has been built across this space, which keeps the room beyond visible and light flowing through, while also creating a home for a record player, LPs and favourite objects.

ABOVE RIGHT The owners of this home have brought the rustic look indoors by reproducing shapes from nature on custom-designed features. The floor in the kitchen has a hand-cut pattern of leaves, created using two different colours of cork tile.

OPPOSITE This cosy living space is brimming with retro rustic ingredients, including an imposing stone fireplace and dark wooden flooring, laid on the diagonal.

in an open–plan space to integrated sideboards, these items are part of the complex fabric of a retro rustic home, bridging the gap between structural component and functional, freestanding furniture.

Plenty of natural and artificial light is essential to the success of any retro rustic space. Dark wood, brick and stone all soak up light, but strategically placed ceiling and wall lamps will offset the gloom and pick out the textures and colours in these natural materials. Keep window treatments to a minimum, too, but where necessary, look for something simple. Vertical blinds have a nicely retro feel, while simple rollers made from wicker rather than fabric are both natural and pretty, gently filtering sunlight.

All this rugged, sensual abundance could feel a little overpowering, but decorative displays, from a stack of books to a pot of wooden spoons, are peppered throughout a retro rustic scheme to guard against overkill. Vintage artwork, potted plants and hand–thrown ceramics in vibrant turquoise and grass green punctuate the look, leading the eye away from the grand backdrop, and towards something more intimate. Retro rustic also loves a quirky collection or handmade object. When dotted throughout a home, they gently personalize this decadent, dramatic look.

DETAILS

TEXTURES

In the modern rustic home, texture brings rich variety, both visual and sensory, to every space. From the knotty wood of ceiling rafters to the softness of a mohair throw, there is much to delight the senses. Bringing the outside in is crucial, so work a host of natural materials into your living space, from wood and wicker to stone and sheepskin. Remember, though, that less can be more when it comes to creating rooms that look and feel great, too. The combination of log-wood furniture, woolly throws and antlers above the fireplace found in rustic interiors of old produced a look that was heavy and dark. Modern rustic has no relationship with that backwoods style. It is lighter, bolder and cleaner, with a well-judged balance of natural, sensual textures.

ABOVE The bathroom in this converted farm building is full of texture, from the brickwork on the walls to the wooden bathtub. This room was originally the place for cheese making, so the owner chose a bathtub reminiscent of the vats used in this process.
OPPOSITE, ABOVE LEFT The black wood of this table is a strong contrast to the objects placed on it – here, some papery-husked tomatillos.

OPPOSITE, ABOVE RIGHT Using different textures, such as sheepskin and linen, increases the tactile appeal of this sofa.
OPPOSITE, BELOW LEFT Small glass handles provide a sparkly contrast to the reclaimed wood on these kitchen drawers.
OPPOSITE, BELOW RIGHT A brilliant way to securely stack logs, layering them in different directions also creates visual interest, turning fuel into a thing of beauty.

Initially, a modern rustic scheme takes inspiration from the textures within the house itself. Anything from an exposed brick wall to a smooth wooden floor will form a rich, organic backdrop. The trick is not to obscure a good thing. Let a stone wall sing out and leave a steel support in place as the proud centrepiece of a space rather than boxing it in. Give any existing feature, in all its tactile glory, room to breathe and your home will feel beautifully uncontrived and grounded.

You can then build up more texture, or inject it into a featureless space, by seeking out interesting materials. Tadelakt, for example, is an ancient, polished lime plaster originally used in Moroccan hammams. It is water resistant and can be used to add soft texture to any wall. For bathrooms and kitchens, hunt down hand-glazed tiles that have irregular surfaces, creating an interesting, uneven finish. Consider fixing tongue-and-groove panelling to walls to give them a Scandinavian vibe, or make a bold statement by cladding a feature wall with reclaimed timber.

RIGHT Reclaimed timber, in a range of finishes and colours, has been pieced and fitted together to create a striking wall and ceiling on the landing of this Californian home. Wood can swallow up light, making a space feel dark, but here, windows, a roof light and the open nature of the landing itself, with views over the dining table below, keep the space bright. A vintage bus blind/shade makes a strong, graphic artwork.

Animal hides are another versatile option much used in modern rustic homes. They are the ultimate natural material and introduce mountains of pleasing texture. Choose between cowhides, which are exceptionally durable, super-soft sheepskin and reindeer hide, which is insulating and, when silicone-cured, waterproof, so it can be used outside as well as in. Use them as rugs, of course, but also as throws, cushion covers or bedspreads. Their benefits stretch beyond the aesthetic. As a natural by-product of the meat-producing industry, hides are abundant and eco-friendly, too.

Modern rustic gains much of its character by mixing the rough with the smooth, so have fun contrasting textures. Spread a sheepskin over a smooth concrete floor or pop a polished aluminium lamp on a knotty wooden desk. Avoid overkill, though. Too much wood, too many sheepskins, and your home will feel cluttered and dull. Restraint is vital. A controlled use of texture will helpfully knock off any masculine edges, but plenty of uncluttered, open space is also crucial to keep the modern sitting comfortably alongside the rustic.

OPPOSITE Stone and brick give this Los Angeles home, built in the 1940s, heaps of grit and solidity. Decorative details – a collection of wooden dolls and some ceramics made by the owner – are kept to a minimum, so that the impressive and striking raw materials are allowed to take centre stage.

ABOVE LEFT This wood, in a converted Dutch farm building, was originally part of the flooring, hand decorated with a diamond pattern by the farm's owners from long ago. When the owners renovated the property, they salvaged these decorative planks and reinvented them as wall panelling.

ABOVE CENTRE & RIGHT Wood, stone and brickwork are favoured in modern rustic homes for their ability to add texture, personality and colour to a space. Wood can be light and clean looking, like this simple ply cladding, while bricks can be laid in a pattern so that texture, colour and decoration combine.

TEXTILES

Modern rustic style makes great use of textiles. They are central to the liveability of this look, adding essential softness to the earthy raw materials that often make up a space. Any natural fabric or material suits a modern rustic scheme, and those with weight and durability are ideal. So use silks and muslins sparingly and favour cool cottons, heavy linens and soft velvet instead. Tactile woven, knitted and worked items, from a mohair throw to a felted place mat, also fit in well. Stick to natural colours, too, but steer clear of the browns and terracottas beloved of traditional rustic schemes. Charcoal greys and soft beiges are more appropriate, creating a sophisticated, neutral backdrop, while flashes of pomegranate red, mossy green or even egg-yolk yellow will create welcome contrast.

ABOVE This sofa is upholstered in a dramatic fabric, with images of birds and moths in deep, dark colours. It creates a welcome, complementary corner of detail against grey walls and dark boards.

OPPOSITE, ABOVE LEFT Strips of different woods, in various tones and finishes, have been laid together to create the attractive patchwork cladding in this eating space.

OPPOSITE, ABOVE RIGHT Velvet is a classic upholstery material. Here, a mossy green tone suits this muted, rustic room.

OPPOSITE, BELOW LEFT A harmonious mix of natural materials – wood, wool, leather and animal hide – sit together.

OPPOSITE, BELOW RIGHT Baskets woven from natural materials such as rush and wicker make good-looking homes for anything from logs to wool scarves.

OPPOSITE Homemade benches topped off with Ikea mattresses form the base of this cosy seating corner. Shaggy sheepskin throws conceal the mattresses, while cotton and linen-covered cushions line the walls, providing back support and extra comfort.

CLOCKWISE FROM TOP LEFT Black and white are a can't-fail combination, but here a fluffy black sheepskin makes a textural contrast to the neatly upholstered white sofa. A simple fringed throw on a day bed. Sleek black leather is softened by a thick knitted throw.

Slubby linen and cotton throws make ideal covers for a simple sofa. Cotton is the perfect rustic choice for simply tied-back curtains/ drapes. Cushion covers made from textural fabrics, casually stitched and finished, look softly rustic.

ABOVE An old armchair has been covered with a knitted woollen throw, perhaps to hide damage to its upholstery or a dated pattern. A cushion, also boasting a chunky wool cover, and a shaggy sheepskin piled on top add layers of texture and softly obscure the shape of the chair so that it looks comfortable, warm and welcoming.

There are millions of different textiles available today, from heavy printed curtain/drape fabric to jewel-bright silks. The abundance can be bewildering, but when creating a modern rustic scheme, you can narrow your choices down quite simply. Begin by eliminating any man-made textiles. Polyesters and nylons strike an inauthentic note. Instead, steer your search towards natural textiles, and think creatively, too. Vintage offcuts or retro curtains/drapes are widely available and inexpensive, and can be reinvented as cushion or seat covers.

Heavy, organic fabrics regularly feature in modern rustic schemes, with everything from bedding to towels and napkins made from thick linen. Look out for familiar materials such as cotton that have been woven or knitted in exciting, unusual ways, creating a textile with character and a tactile quality. Hand-embroidered textiles are also a lovely addition, brimming with texture and a bohemian, folksy feel, while the odd surprise textile, such as colourful silk on a cushion cover, brings a flash of contrast.

Patterned textiles add pockets of detail to a gritty backdrop, but they are only ever used minimally. Classic designs in earthy colours, from plaids to paisleys, work best; there is no place for cheerful polka dots or candy stripes in a modern rustic home! Think Welsh blankets, contemporary tartan, Indian kilims or patterns that reference the natural world in a bold, striking way. Just remember that any design must hold its own against the rough surfaces and deep colours of a rustic room, and this demands a level of sophistication and drama.

THIS PAGE Vintage-style velvet in a variety of watery colours covers this modular sofa, while cushions in contrasting textiles, including crochet and felt, are scattered across it to create a rich mix of texture, fabric and colour. The turquoise notes on the textiles and buttons are also picked up in the painting hanging on the wall behind.

FURNITURE

Many kinds of furniture suit a modern rustic home. Family heirlooms, upcycled pieces, classic mid-century design and even the odd contemporary find can all be used to great effect. Although sourced from different outlets and eras, these pieces will share certain traits. Each one is beautifully designed, predominantly made from natural materials and endowed with earthy personality so that it looks neither boring nor ornate.

Although there are no rules about where to pick up furniture, it is helpful to restrict your search by sticking to a palette of uniform colours and materials. Remember, also, to keep one foot on the brakes when it comes to how much you buy. Filling a room with furniture of all shapes and sizes will drive the modern feel from this rustic look.

ABOVE Vintage leather armchairs with a rich patina are positioned around a sheepskin rug, creating a comfortable hub, with original built-in storage and shelves further zoning this space as a corner to read or relax in.

OPPOSITE, ABOVE LEFT This Ekstrem chair by Terje Ekstrøm for Variér was designed in the 1980s and is still in production today. It combines striking design and ergonomics, and stands out beautifully against this panelled wall.

OPPOSITE, ABOVE RIGHT A Papermaster magazine rack, designed by Torbjørn Anderssen for Swedese, stands against a curving wall in this Norwegian home.

OPPOSITE, BELOW LEFT Padded arms and cushions make this leather lounge chair, designed by Harald Relling in the 1970s, both comfortable and stylish.

OPPOSITE, BELOW RIGHT Designed by Dan Johnson in the 1950s, this Gazelle chair is rare and collectable.

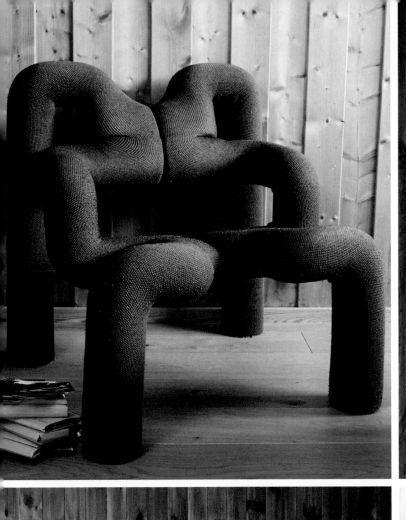

If you are buying new furniture, go for understated pieces. The design should be spare and simple; neither sleekly modern nor ornate and antique. Mid-range high-street retailers have an abundant stock of sofas, armchairs, beds and footstools with the kind of softly modern lines that perfectly suit a modern rustic home. Before you buy, though, look beyond the piece's form and consider function and feel, too. Is that sofa practical and comfortable, as well as good looking? Is it available in a quality, durable fabric? Will it fit into your home?

Older pieces are also welcome in a modern rustic room, whether they are lucky car-boot/ yard-sale finds or classic designs. Look out for furniture that is light, elegant and even austere to stand out against the raw materials on show. Mid-century design is a great option in a home already boasting a rustic backdrop of wood, stone and brick – its clean lines are a nice contrast. In a more neutral home, opt for pieces

with weight and presence, from heavy benches to capacious cupboards, but think rustic not farmhouse when choosing. Stick to simple shapes and avoid fussy detailing or paint finishes.

Fleamarkets, fairs and auctions are good hunting grounds for rustic pieces, but finds may need a little loving care to reach their full potential. So long as the structure is sound, any wooden piece can be improved by sanding off and sealing with wax or matt varnish. Similarly, sofas and chairs with worn covers or exploding stuffing can be reupholstered for a fresh look.

Finally, consider having furniture built in. This makes efficient use of space and can transform even the most awkward corner into invaluable storage, leaving the rest of the room uncluttered. You have control over the materials, finish and colour, too. In addition, you benefit from the craftsman's or designer's experience. He or she may suggest inspired ways to work further modern rustic touches into your home.

ABOVE LEFT These pots, made from ceramic and woven natural fibres, were created by the owner of this home. Here, they are displayed on a neat rustic coffee table.
ABOVE CENTRE With its reindeer-hide seat, this classic lounge chair is already comfortable, but a woollen throw adds some contrasting texture.
ABOVE RIGHT Woven natural fibre matting or rugs are a durable and attractive modern rustic floor covering.
OPPOSITE Despite the abundance of rustic natural materials in this comfortable corner, the space still has a strongly retro feel thanks to the artwork, chair and the mid-century sideboard.

LIGHTING

Lighting in a modern rustic scheme needs serious consideration. When natural materials are used abundantly, a space can look stark and forbidding. Raw surfaces and deep, matt colours tend to swallow light, too, so ample sources of both natural and artificial light are vital to compensate for this. Planning a lighting scheme can be complex, but as a basic rule, aim to work in a good mix of lighting 'types'. The three key 'types' are ambient lighting, which provides the overall illumination; task lighting, which is strong, directional light; and accent lighting, which picks out a particular object or feature. Most modern rustic rooms rely on plenty of ambient light – usually wall and ceiling lights, plus the odd stylish lamp – teamed with task lighting over work stations.

ABOVE A metal pole with a hook at the top is set into a solid block of wood to form the basis for this simple, rustic floor lamp. An industrial-style light is then suspended from the hook.

OPPOSITE, ABOVE LEFT Pretty antiqued silver tealight holders, suspended on wires from the ceiling, look good whether the candles are lit or not.

OPPOSITE, ABOVE RIGHT A hook, some antique-style flex and a statement bulb make a simple but effective wall light.

OPPOSITE, BELOW LEFT A collection of monochrome candles and tealights is clustered together to create a glow of ambient light in the centre of this solid, rustic table.

OPPOSITE, BELOW RIGHT The clean lines of this modernist white light stand out beautifully against the wood-panelled wall.

LEFT This lampshade, hanging dramatically over a dining table, was created by the owner of the house.
BELOW LEFT Simple wall lights installed along this corridor are given a quirky, rustic feel with the addition of deer antlers fitted below.
RIGHT A classic globe light looks appealing when illuminated.

Your lighting 'recipe' will alter room by room, depending on how and when each space is used. Bedrooms, for example, need a mix of ambient light for dressing, task lighting for bedtime reading and softer light for relaxing, while a bathroom needs a similar combination, but here lighting must be carefully assessed for safety, depending on its proximity to water and moisture.

A good number of built-in ceiling lights will create a backdrop of ambient light in the rooms that see most activity – the kitchen and living space – and these can be supplemented by freestanding lamps. The classic anglepoise light is a handsome option, which offers directional light, too. Shop around for an original, vintage design or find a modern take on this classic style on the high street. Lamps with coloured glass or ceramic bases add welcome brightness and can be topped with a neutral shade for balance. Scour fleamarkets for anything vintage and eye-catching, and don't be put off if a lamp needs rewiring. It is a relatively simple task and there are plenty of DIY demonstrations online to help.

Lighting is highly functional, but it can also bring drama and glamour to a space, so remember to work in a handful of lights that both work hard and look gorgeous.

THIS PAGE Hanging a striking ceiling light low over a dining table is a tried and trusted idea, but here the wicker shade creates a strongly retro rustic feel. When the light is on, its woven design casts interesting patterns across the white walls.

RESCUED & RECYCLED

Today, all kinds of interior styles champion the use of rescued and recycled pieces. There is something incredibly satisfying about giving old furniture, lighting and decorative objects a new home, and their uniqueness brings distinct character to any space. Using recycled pieces is environmentally responsible, too – why buy new when there are so many interesting objects already in existence? – and these finds are often wonderfully inexpensive. The only danger in raiding a junk shop is that your home can end up resembling one! In fact, many schemes featuring pre-loved items rock a look of battered informality, but not the modern rustic space. Instead, a carefully selected assortment of second-hand materials and finds are used sparingly and innovatively for a crisper, more designed effect.

ABOVE A rescued piece of industrial storage is now attractive open shelving in this cabin kitchen. New wooden shelves have been added, contrasting beautifully with the beaten-up metal.
OPPOSITE, ABOVE LEFT Salvage yards and vintage stores are just one source of recycled pieces; the great outdoors is another! This shapely piece of tree branch has been reinvented as a candle holder.

OPPOSITE, ABOVE RIGHT A Japanese tea cup is used as a vessel for pretty cutlery/flatware.
OPPOSITE, BELOW LEFT Small logs have been painted grey and hollowed out to accommodate a tealight, creating a striking display in this fireplace.
OPPOSITE, BELOW RIGHT This rustic coffee table has been constructed from a section of tree trunk topped with a square of concrete.

LEFT This dramatic light fixture was made bespoke for the space from a tree branch and a row of bulbs on sculpted metal.
BELOW LEFT Salvaged picture frames make appealing surrounds for these botanical prints, which are fixed directly to the wall.
RIGHT An old barometer predicts the weather.

Incorporating rescued and recycled pieces into a modern rustic home involves more than just dotting a few fleamarket buys around. Instead, explore the world of architectural salvage. Wooden parquet, stone flags, old cast-iron radiators and antique panelling can all be integrated into a modern rustic space, bringing welcome texture and warmth.

Do not imagine you need to hire a van to visit a salvage yard, though; there are always plenty of small objects in stock that will bring a rustic touch to your scheme. Weathered metal handles are a nice contrast on newly built-in storage, while enamelled door numbers make a handsome display. New roles can be devised for uninspiring raw materials, too. Simple timber planks can be sanded and sealed to make a basin surround or shelf, while wooden flooring can become a timber feature wall.

Most modern rustic schemes incorporate a few pieces of contemporary furniture, which you won't find in a fleamarket, but keep an eye out for any dramatic one-offs, though – a chandelier or striking cabinet – then enjoy picking up smaller items that fit the modern rustic mood, from chunky pottery to silver cutlery/flatware; battered baskets to misty mirrors.

Look beyond each object's original purpose and think of new, creative ways to use it. Earthenware pots can serve as cutlery/flatware storage, an old lobster pot can become a hanging display or lampshade, while industrial wire baskets make perfect shoe or log storage. A little imagination is all that is needed.

LEFT The attractive panelling by the front door of this Dutch home was also originally floorboards. Previous owners would have made inexpensive wood look more attractive by decorating it with this diamond pattern.

ABOVE A wall of built-in wardrobes/cutom-built closets makes great use of the space in the master bedroom of this Dutch home. The wood used for the doors was originally flooring downstairs.

ON DISPLAY

Display is central to many interior decorating styles, but modern rustic likes to keep things simple. Generally, it is the room, its architecture and the surfaces and textures within it that are the star attractions and decorative items are kept to a minimum. Lots of 'stuff' against a raw, earthy backdrop will at best distract from the main event and at worst look muddled, cluttered and confusing. Instead, artworks, photographs, personal treasures and trinkets are displayed only where they are not in competition with the backdrop they stand against. The trick is to choose the objects, and their location, very carefully. Keep to a uniform recipe and try to carry the same colours and materials from room to room, for a pleasing feeling of cohesion and calm.

ABOVE The owner of this home makes jewellery, and many of her designs are displayed here in a handsome metal cabinet. Hung at different depths, the necklaces are safely stored – no risk of tangles – and beautifully displayed.

OPPOSITE, ABOVE LEFT Simple wooden boxes find a new role as shelves for display when hung on the wall in this bathroom.

OPPOSITE, ABOVE RIGHT All sorts of items can make a striking display, from an artist's hand model to a peg doll.

OPPOSITE, BELOW LEFT Instead of living in a drawer, these metal scissors look gorgeous hung against a grey wall.

OPPOSITE, BELOW RIGHT Hanging necklaces and accessories from a peg rail allows you to see and enjoy your jewellery collection when not wearing it.

Modern rustic is not a minimalist look, but display is nevertheless managed carefully. Natural materials, used so often in a modern rustic home, are also found on the items displayed within it. These should share a bond with the natural world and with the materials the house is constructed from. So choose pieces with soul, made from wood, earthenware, glass and wicker, and avoid anything artificial, kitsch or over-designed. Think about the impact of any display, too. Small groups of similar objects work best, adding interest but not clutter to a space.

Colour occasionally crops up on the pieces displayed in a modern rustic scheme, but it is only dotted here and there to punctuate a space. Turquoise, green and mustard tones fit in and are often found on pottery, lamp bases or kitchenware. Books make another colourful yet low-key display and can be stacked flat, rather than upright, for some visual variety.

Items that come straight from the natural world are prime candidates for display. Think antlers, polished animal horns and house plants. Carved items, from figurines to hefty platters, keep this look's love affair with wood alive, while vintage oddities or souvenirs from distant travels will bring personality to your space.

Use your imagination, too, and see the beauty in everyday objects. Pick up feathers, seashells, driftwood and pine cones when exploring outdoors, and then display them creatively. All kinds of unlikely bits and bobs become mini works of art once cleaned up and positioned thoughtfully.

ABOVE This striking storage unit holds books and decorative objects, while its wooden doors cleverly conceal a television. It was built centrally, with glass windows seeming to wrap around it and the woodwork on the garden wall beyond visible.
OPPOSITE This striking old cabinet is home to a huge array of curios and objects, from clocks to ceramics. Big collections like this can become dusty, but keeping them in glass-fronted storage protects them.

THIS PAGE & OPPOSITE A casual display of found objects, sketches and photos hangs on this wall for an organic feel that fits with the textiles and materials in the house.

ROOMS

LEFT A hanging cane chair is a retro staple, but painted black it has a more timeless, urban feel.

RIGHT Seating is essential in any living space, but here a mixture of a modular sofa and built-in bench brings welcome variety. Armfuls of cushions turn a fireside alcove into a cosy reading spot, with space for log storage below.

LIVING ROOMS

Today, informal entertaining, work, study and family time often take place in the kitchen. A table and chairs, perhaps an armchair, too, are all that is needed to transform what was once a space devoted to cooking into a valuable family hub. This means that the living room has evolved into more of a retreat; somewhere to relax, watch TV and cuddle up on a sofa with the children. It needs to be comfortable and calm but, as it may also be used for socializing, quickly able to smarten itself up for public scrutiny when guests arrive. Modern rustic style, with its emphasis on organic ingredients and unpretentious finishes, brings a warm, inviting feel to this crucial space, ensuring it is ordered, elegant and inviting at any time of day.

ABOVE LEFT Ethnic patterns on the rug and cushions add detail, while their rich colours contrast nicely with the deep green of the sofa.

ABOVE RIGHT & OPPOSITE A flowing configuration and glass doors that pull open create a living space that blurs the boundaries between inside and out.

LEFT Dark wood and flashes of turquoise ramp up the style in this musical corner.

So where to begin? Natural materials are essential to every modern rustic scheme, but if you can weave them into the fabric of your living space, rather than simply dot them around as details, you will create real drama. Scrutinize your living space and see what it has to offer. Are there any ruggedly handsome features, such as a stone fireplace or a beautiful parquet floor? Any existing gems can become the driver of your scheme, and you can then build the incidentals of furniture and display around them.

Try to see the potential of any elements that may once have been considered ugly or

LEFT Low shelves fit neatly along this wall and provide space for display as well as storage. Lying books on their sides (and organizing them by colour) creates pleasing stacks and horizontal lines. Here, some piles are home to favourite objects in addition to the pots that the owner makes.
BELOW This simple living space has a dramatic black painted wall, against which a boxy, modern sofa with a white slip cover sits. The photographs hanging above it are by artist Zoe Crosher.

unsophisticated, too. Often, a little room to breathe is all that is needed to take a solid architectural detail such as a fireplace or beam from heavy to heavenly. Once combined with calming colours and unfussy furniture, it is more likely to look attractive. Alternatively, give a stand-out feature a makeover, to help it look its best. Brick, for example, can be painted so that it appears to melt into its surroundings, while still bringing welcome texture to a wall.

Modern rustic likes to step outside the conventional decorating box and is always looking for exciting ways to bring the outside into a home – no matter what its style or age. Consider cladding walls with timber. It can look either wonderfully rustic or silky and sophisticated, and even just a single clad wall will give a living space a dramatic edge. Red cedar is a sustainably grown softwood that is lightweight and suitable for use inside, with a straight grain and uniform

OPPOSITE Brick walls, wood-clad ceilings, a stone fireplace – this living space has lots of rustic elements and they are all original features, dating from the 1940s. The owner made the sofa in a woodworking class, then added cushions and a sheepskin.

ABOVE LEFT Built-in storage helps keep this small living room tidy and makes efficient use of the available space. A leather corner sofa sits neatly against two walls to leave maximum floor space exposed, and introduces a softly rustic note, too.

ABOVE RIGHT A classic Ercol sofa is given a rustic feel when layered with sheepskins and folksy, embroidered cushions. Their bright colours punctuate a backdrop of reclaimed wood on the walls.

texture. For a more rugged look, source timber from a reclamation yard. It will come in a variety of finishes, producing a richly textured effect.

Play around with lines and perspective. Timber planks don't need to be hung vertically; you could try cladding walls in overlapping horizontal panels fixed to a framework of battens, called shiplap. Horizontal lines have the effect of widening a space, but there are other benefits to using wood on your walls. Wood has excellent sound-insulation properties and will hide a poor-quality surface or ceiling. It's also a good solution if you want to install integrated lighting, as it can conceal wiring and electrics.

If this all sounds too structural, fake it! Cheat with lightweight, interlocking brick-effect panels. These are typically made from

durable polyurethane, marble powder and resin for a realistic finish. You simply screw the panels, which can be cut to size, to your wall. (See Sources on pages 156–7 for stockists.)

Wallpaper is another neat cheat that will bring a blast of rusticity to your living room. There are hundreds of trompe l'oeil papers available designed to look like building materials, from regular red bricks to chunky stones and skinny black slate. Some are even lightly textured for greater authenticity. Look out, also, for wood grain papers in a range of timber tones. If you find this a little artificial, take heart. Used sparingly when the real thing is not available, these papers introduce a rustic note and are affordable, quick to hang and easily updated when you fancy a change.

Elsewhere in the living space, smoothly plastered walls will prove a good foil to gritty features. Choose colours that sit at the pale, muted end of the paint chart, and don't rule out simple, fresh white – a perfect fit for a contemporary rustic scheme where pops of bright play against wood and stone. Consider dark shades, too. Mushroom, stormy blue, moss green and plum come straight from nature. Deep grey is another modern rustic favourite. Paint it on a feature wall or, if your living space is blessed with ample natural light, use it everywhere to give the room an enveloping feel.

If you are renovating your home and need to replaster, consider using a softly pigmented plaster. This sidesteps the need to paint the walls and creates a finish with depth and a sense of texture that is perfectly in keeping with modern rustic style. The ancient Moroccan plaster finish tadelakt is another option. It has a warm look, bursting with texture, and can be tinted in a range of earthy tones. Or try lime

ABOVE RIGHT & RIGHT Wrapping paper has been pasted to the glass wall in this apartment, to provide privacy for what is now a bedroom on the other side.
LEFT Modern rustic loves to bring the outside into each room, and house plants are an easy way to introduce a touch of organic, living green to a space. Here, an old can has been recycled and used as a plant pot.

THIS PAGE Painting this wall black gives it real impact and helps to frame the dramatic fireplace. Cleverly stacked logs and displays of branches and tree trunks bring the outside in.

BELOW A rustic child's bed, now used as a day bed, is the perfect place to enjoy the view.

BELOW RIGHT Silk, satin or bright cushions don't work in a rustic scheme. Instead, choose knitted covers, crumply linen or cotton in natural tones.

LEFT A cosy corner in this Norwegian cabin is home to a small, rustic table and chairs where children can draw or play. Sheepskins and cushions soften up a bench built along the wall, while the combination of black walls and white flooring lends a distinctly Scandinavian feel.

OPPOSITE There are no freestanding sofas in this Norwegian cabin. Instead, the owners have built simple bench seating into the corners of the living space, covered with Ikea mattresses and layered up with sheepskins and cushions. Colours are muted, but patterns and stripes help create depth.

Weaving in plenty of
texture keeps the grey,
black and white colour
scheme in this newly
built barn-style home
feeling elegant rather
than stark. A black

sheepskin adds tactile
depth to a simple white
sofa, while three moody
Shipwreck prints by
Leah Fusco and a steel
anglepoise lamp contrast
with the knotty wood of
the industrial-style bench.

RIGHT Forget logs stacked
in a basket; this is a
more original, sculptural
fireside piece. Antlers
and horns have been
tumbled into a black
bucket, made from
recycled car tyres.

paint, which has been used for thousands of
years and produces a nuanced finish. It is made
from quick lime and natural pigments, making
it an ecological option.

When building in a feature such as a
fireplace, explore the contemporary side of
modern rustic style and consider a material such
as concrete. Hard-wearing and good-looking,
it can be made with a polished, rough, silk
or matt finish. Polished concrete is also a great
option for living room flooring, introducing
a pared-back, minimal feel. Alternatively, stick
to a more traditional wooden floor, but keep
an eye open for exciting contrasts. Pale wide
boards make a cool backdrop for textural,
timber-clad walls, for example, while boards
painted black create a striking contrast to
stripped wooden furniture.

Curtains/drapes or blinds/shades are
essential for privacy and insulation in a living
space, but keep them simple. Heavy linen
curtains/drapes in an oatmeal tone will work
in almost any style of modern rustic living
room, although if your tastes lean more to
the bohemian, pick a gently patterned fabric
in soft colours. Choose a material with weight
and texture, too, which can hold its own

against the raw ingredients of the room and boost its earthy feel. Be generous with fabric quantities. Richly gathered curtains/drapes add a welcome shot of luxury that softens the raw, rough materials of a modern rustic space. Just make sure they do not obscure daylight. A modern rustic scheme needs plenty of natural as well as artificial light to prevent it looking oppressive or dull.

When it comes to furniture, explore both the modern and the rustic elements of this look. Guard against the temptation to fill your living space with squishy sofas and shabby footstools, though, in a bid to soften its rough edges. A few cosy elements are welcome, but be brave, steering towards smart, strong styles that will effortlessly preserve the modern feel.

A simple, contemporary sofa upholstered in beige or grey linen will make the perfect

ABOVE These 1970s design classic chairs by Harald Relling are grouped around a sleek wooden coffee table. The effect could be minimal and modernist, but the worn green leather of the chairs, wooden wall cladding and lush house plants tip the space back towards a modern rustic look.

RIGHT A wood burner stands near the entrance to the open-plan kitchen and dining space in this modern rustic Norwegian home, its dark metal helping it to blend into the wall behind. Bedrooms open off a long corridor beyond, with doors in pale plywood that contrasts with the dark clad walls.

understated addition to a room that boasts strong lines and bold features. You might even like to invest in a design classic, too. Many of the iconic chairs of the 20th century team clean lines with soft leather, striking just the right note of masculine, earthy glamour. Charles and Ray Eames's lounge chair and footstool for Vitra is a great example, while elegant mid-century modern designs by the likes of Hans Wegner combined wooden frames and neat upholstery on seating that still looks highly contemporary today.

You can then layer up your key pieces of furniture with tactile textiles and hides to add texture and a little softness. Look out for

ABOVE Throughout the communal rooms in this Norwegian house, walls are clad with spruce treated with a single coat of charcoal grey stain so that the finish is completely matt and the grain can be seen through it. Light from the tall garden windows helps this space feel dramatic, not dingy.

anything hand-crafted, such as a traditional Welsh blanket, faded antique kilim or woven cotton throw. Animal furs and hides, thrown over sofas and across hard floors, are another lovely addition, bringing natural colour and a super-soft feel.

Remember to explore fleamarkets, junk shops and family attics for furniture gems that will fit in with the modern rustic scheme. Vintage pieces with a slightly raw look, boasting chips, dents and scrapes, will look suitably characterful. In a large living room, a show-stopping antique armoire or simple rustic shelves will flesh things out and provide useful storage, but aim to keep the space

RIGHT & BELOW A large-scale room like the living space in this Dutch home demands large-scale decoration. A huge, rustic table is home to a collection of heavy stone vessels. The branches of blossom add a feminine focal point.

FAR RIGHT Decorative objects are kept to a minimum in this beautifully styled house so that its original features and traditional materials command the attention. A refined palette, teamed with a variety of textures, makes the space soothing but not dull.

reasonably uncluttered so that the natural materials and the room's architecture can be enjoyed.

When it comes to styling your space, exercise restraint. Raw, rough features need only subtle embellishment and adding too many colourful knick-knacks will harm the serious, sensual feel of your space. The odd decorative object, carefully positioned, will personalize the room, but avoid clutter at all costs.

Choose objects in those materials that already feature, such as wood, to keep the look calm and cohesive. Leave walls bare or hang artwork that can stand up against this moody backdrop. Black and white photography brings a contemporary edge, while images taken from nature – butterflies, leaves, flowers – and even abstract modern art in warm, muted tones will work. Or simply weave in wood in its most basic state – as logs, dramatically stacked to the ceiling in an alcove or tumbled into a huge fireside basket.

OPPOSITE Many rooms have seating and furniture arranged to look towards the fireplace, but here, chairs are positioned around an oblong, rustic table to make the most of the room's length.

COOKING & EATING

Perhaps no room in the house has changed as dramatically over the last half century as the kitchen. Once a purely practical space that only the cook spent time in, today's kitchens are sociable, multi-tasking places where we eat, entertain and relax. They contain equipment and technology, from ovens to extractor fans, work surfaces for food preparation and some kind of dining space, too, if we can squeeze it in, for happy gatherings, busy breakfasts and homework sessions. This space must offer great functionality, but everything should also look good, from the cupboards to the crockery. Luckily, the modern rustic kitchen can rise to this challenge. Clutter-free yet full of character, it is well designed, easy to live with and so much more interesting than a standard white kitchen.

ABOVE, LEFT & RIGHT Simple wooden shelves and ceramic pots keep kitchen kit to hand, while also creating an informal display.
RIGHT Chunky earthenware in sludgy tones and tactile linen napkins perfectly suit this modern rustic home.
OPPOSITE The kitchen in this Norwegian cabin is a harmonious mix of various rustic materials and finishes, from the reclaimed wood used to make the cupboards to the plaster-effect treatment on the walls.

THIS PAGE Clever design tricks have been used to zone this large open-plan space. The white floorboards change to chunky tiling where the cooking space begins, while low-slung ceiling pendants hang over the table, creating a hub bathed in warm light for cosy meal times.

ABOVE LEFT You could never mistake this space for a cottage kitchen, yet it shares many of the same ingredients. There is an Aga, brick walls and earthenware containers holding utensils, but these rustic staples are teamed with modern task lighting, reclaimed woods and a powder-coated steel plate behind the range, for a contemporary feel.

ABOVE RIGHT The cabinet panelling is reclaimed oak from French railway carriages/railroad cars.

OPPOSITE This kitchen sits within an extension off a 17th-century cottage in Scotland. What was originally the exterior wall is now incorporated as a rugged interior wall. The large island unit is made from reclaimed wood.

The modern rustic cooking space loves to mix old and new – whether that means fitting a modern kitchen in an ancient building or combining state-of-the-art technology with antique furniture and reclaimed floorboards. Contrast is key. Forget matchy-matchy or minimalist styles and revel in the juxtaposition of rough and smooth, industrial and folky.

Rather than source your entire kitchen and dining space from the same supplier, take a mix and match approach and seek out furniture, tiling and surfaces from different outlets and makers for a truly bespoke look. There is nothing wrong with buying a simple white kitchen from the high street either, but you could then combine it in interesting ways with freestanding pieces and characterful flooring and work surfaces. Remember, too, that a good fitter can make even inexpensive units look beautiful, so track down someone with experience and skill.

It is a good idea to collect samples first, to make sure treatments and materials work well together. Keep your eyes open when out and about for exciting combinations. Lots of restaurants and bars have their kitchens on view, so if you see a mix of surfaces and colours that you like, note it down. You can also base your look on something

THIS PAGE Contrasting woods and plenty of natural light give this open-plan kitchen and dining space bags of style and a welcoming feel, too. The generous proportions of the room mean the table becomes a focal point, rather than a squeezed-in addition.

LEFT Simple leather straps, attached to the top lip of each drawer, have been used as an original alternative to handles or knobs in this kitchen. They add a quirky, rustic touch and subtly break up the run of black units.

you have seen in this book or in a magazine. Rip out tear sheets and collate in a scrapbook, or gather your ideas on a Pinterest board. Alternatively, simply base your look on something you already own, whether that is a single plate or a beautiful wooden table.

If you are designing the cooking and eating space from scratch, it is important to go beyond aesthetics. Consider how many people will use it and when. Will this simply be a place to cook and give the kids breakfast in, or will you be entertaining in here, too? A straightforward breakfast bar is easy to fit into any space, but incorporating a freestanding island or large table will take more planning. Remember to always factor in this room's practical role and make sure the plans you have for it do not hinder its functionality.

In terms of configuration, generally speaking, seating should be at a distance from the busiest part of the kitchen so that people are not in the way while you are cooking. A classic kitchen table is the simplest way to create an eating area. It is also a non-permanent feature that can easily be shifted. Just make sure there is at least a metre/yard of floor

ABOVE RIGHT These kitchen units were made using ply, stained black and teamed with a marble splashback. The cabinet doors above were made from white Perspex with holes for handles.

RIGHT Classic Wishbone chairs, designed by Hans Wegner for Carl Hansen, are a timeless addition to this elegant room, their honey-toned wood striking against the dark background.

LEFT & BELOW Recycled material has been used to transform a bland 1960s property into a home brimming with personality. Larch wood cladding on the kitchen cabinets brings nature in and is brightened with mismatched glass handles. The wood came from trees blown down in Kew Gardens during the hurricane of 1987. The work surface is made from crushed, recycled glass, with bits of mirror mixed in to add sparkle.

OPPOSITE Cupboards faced with waxed larch teamed with a dramatic, vintage cabinet – filled with an eclectic collection of tableware – adds great personality to this kitchen. New oak flooring keeps things sleek underfoot.

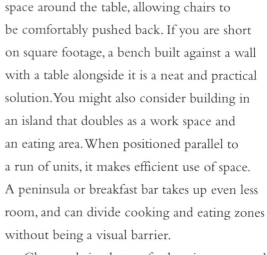

space around the table, allowing chairs to be comfortably pushed back. If you are short on square footage, a bench built against a wall with a table alongside it is a neat and practical solution. You might also consider building in an island that doubles as a work space and an eating area. When positioned parallel to a run of units, it makes efficient use of space. A peninsula or breakfast bar takes up even less room, and can divide cooking and eating zones without being a visual barrier.

Choose chairs that perfectly suit your strand of modern rustic. Elegant mid-century designs with waspish waists suit a pop rustic scheme, while a simple wooden bench looks perfect in a pure rustic setting. Chairs with padded seats allow you to incorporate upholstery and different textures in your dining space, to create a warm, inviting feel. You could also re-cover existing seat pads in a more vibrant material for a shot of brightness amongst the rusticity.

When choosing materials for your kitchen, think about functionality as well as appearance. Counter tops are the hardest-working surface, so must perform well and look great, too. As different areas will serve different functions, you could use a mix of surfaces. Choose something

THIS PAGE Plain units and a pale work surface create a neutral backdrop for the rustic furniture in this kitchen. A farmhouse-style table spread with a linen cloth and teamed with simple benches is the centrepiece, while space around is clear – even the range stands alone, with no cupboards flanking it.

durable where food preparation takes place – stainless steel, for example – and an accent surface for an island or peninsula. In a small kitchen, you may prefer to keep the work surfaces the same, for a sense of continuity.

Wooden work surfaces bring a touch of rustic warmth and can help link the kitchen with other furniture in the room and beyond, but don't be afraid to use a more contemporary material. This will combine functionality with sleek good looks and can be easily steered towards the rustic by dotting it with earthy accessories and attractive kitchen kit. Composites like Corian are sturdy and can be joined invisibly, with sinks and upstands integrated. Engineered or composite stone, meanwhile, is typically made of crushed quartz mixed with resin. Tough and low maintenance, it's ideal for use throughout your cooking space and comes in a wide range of colours.

Concrete is the ultimate contemporary material. It is extremely durable and can be polished to give a super-smooth feel. It will sit happily alongside other surfaces such as wood or stainless steel for an exciting modern rustic look. Whichever work top you choose, consider contrasting it with the units below. Cabinets faced with reclaimed wood against a polished concrete or cool composite work surface create an exciting clash of rough and smooth.

Kitchen flooring should complement the space rather than be the focal point. In a small kitchen, choose a surface that will work throughout the whole area. In a large room, you could opt for a practical material in the

RIGHT Bench seating is arranged around a long table in this modern barn. Simple styling helps this furniture feel both rustic and modern. **BELOW** Wooden chopping boards strike a rustic note against a solid black splashback.

RIGHT A thin, waterproof emulsion in various shades was painted onto this kitchen shelving. It allows the veining of the wood to be seen through it.

FAR RIGHT A wall covered with blackboard paint provides a creative space for children to doodle in chalk.

LEFT A utilitarian kitchen brings a shot of contemporary urban style to this farm building conversion. The black steel workbench and large extractor fan would not look out of place in a professional kitchen, while the open wooden shelving and cabinets behind are a modern take on a rustic pantry.

OPPOSITE Bold colour is a key, modern ingredient of this farm building conversion. The table top is made from a double layer of recycled plywood, lacquered twice in a vibrant orange to create a tough finish. The pendant lampshade is made from a Thai basket used for carrying chickens to market.

FAR LEFT Rich wood is the USP of this kitchen, and to prevent it becoming obscured by a handle, simple and unobtrusive metal pulls are fitted at the top of each drawer.

LEFT Cabinet space is hidden inside a floor-to-ceiling bank of storage for a streamlined look.

OPPOSITE This house has a grand dining space, so this oblong table in the kitchen, with bench seating built around, is for informal meal times.

BELOW The flooring changes from wooden boards to tinted and polished concrete to demarcate the kitchen in this open-plan space.

cooking area, such as tiling or stone, and something more decorative elsewhere. Solid wooden flooring helps to absorb noise, resulting in a calmer environment – ideal in a large, open-plan home, which can have tricky acoustics. Poured flooring such as concrete or resin brings a contemporary edge. If your budget allows, consider underfloor heating, too. It will keep the room cosy and would enable you to remove radiators, making more space for cabinets.

Where lighting is concerned, flexibility is key. This is a space that requires strong task lighting for food preparation, but softer lighting for dining and relaxing. Ideally, fit plenty of ceiling lights and zone different areas of lighting on separate circuits so that they can be controlled independently. Even a simple dimmer switch will help control brightness levels, allowing you to alter the lighting mood. Table lamps and floor lamps are another option in a large space, but beware of trailing flexes, which are a dangerous trip hazard.

Fully integrated appliances, hidden behind sleek doors, are staples of super-sleek, contemporary kitchens, but it is not necessary to conceal them in a modern rustic room. A stainless-steel range will make a strong focal point with a professional feel, and you can cosy up its appearance with warm wood and darker shades elsewhere. Or set an oven

and fridge into a wall of timber-faced cupboards, for a nice clash of colours and materials.

Think imaginatively about the style of storage. A traditional run of base and wall units makes efficient use of space, but you might also like to team built-in furniture with freestanding pieces. Open shelves help a kitchen feel more lived in and allow you to display much-loved china. Larders are another good option. Everything inside can be seen at a glance and, on average, they hold as much as eight wall-mounted kitchen units, but take up less width. In place of a traditional island unit, seek out a freestanding work table that you can prepare food

OPPOSITE, LEFT & ABOVE RIGHT Polished plywood units, stainless-steel work surfaces and exposed breeze/cinder-block walls give the kitchen a sensual and slightly masculine feel.

OPPOSITE, BELOW RIGHT The units that run along one wall in the dining space match those in the kitchen.
BELOW & RIGHT The owner of this LA house, built in 1946, has preserved its original features, which includes lots of panelling! Abundant sunlight helps the kitchen look warm and welcoming, while the ceramics, crafted by the owner, personalize the area.

at, with storage below. Scour salvage yards and eBay for a vintage piece, or consider having a table made to your own specifications.

Natural materials create striking backdrops and bold statements in a modern rustic space, but it's important to consider the small details, too. In a kitchen, finishing touches such as handles can make a huge difference. Handle-less cabinets and drawers look contemporary, while contrasting timber-clad door fronts with tiny glass knobs gives a little sparkle and sweetness to the wood. Just remember to position handles carefully – you don't want them catching on waist-height pockets.

Finally, display a few pieces of kitchen kit that combine form and function beautifully. Whether that is a stack of handmade ceramic bowls or chunky chopping boards leaning against a wall, choose just a handful of fitting objects and arrange them thoughtfully to gently round out your modern rustic space. Search out characterful, classic versions of staples such as coffee pots, casseroles and kettles, avoiding anything super shiny or colourful. Add a few pieces of artwork, too, perhaps just propped up on a work surface, and include flowers, pot plants and herbs for some lush, organic green.

LEFT & RIGHT A wall of integrated storage keeps this bedroom uncluttered and the beautiful grain of the smooth plywood becomes a feature, too. Grey bed linen picks up the colour of the breeze/cinder-block wall, while bedside shelves rather than units keep the floor clear.

BEDROOMS

It is received decorating wisdom that the bedroom is the one space in which you can really experiment. It is a purely personal room, after all, and therefore ripe for self-expression – or so the theory goes. Of course, there is some truth in this. Bedrooms are not open to public scrutiny and are seldom seen by visitors, so they can afford to look different, but in a modern rustic scheme, cohesion is important. The same colours, materials and textiles are used throughout a home to ensure each room flows organically into the next. So stick to the simple, honest ingredients that you have used elsewhere, but take into account the intimate, personal nature of a bedroom and aim for a slightly softer, more romantic result; less raw, more refined.

There is no law, of course, that says you must make your bedroom more feminine than the rest of the house, but if your instinct is to soften up the modern rustic look in here, begin with the flooring. Elsewhere, flooring is almost always hard, but the bedroom is about the only place that can carry off a carpet without seeming to deviate drastically from the style of the other rooms. Opt for a muted colour and be sure to team it with plenty of rustic touches on walls, ceiling and furniture. Wood and brick will work well alongside a soft, pale carpet, but beware a combination of carpet and painted walls. It's simply not rustic enough and smacks of a boutique hotel rather than an earthy retreat!

Wooden flooring is a perfect option in a bedroom, as elsewhere in a modern rustic home. Hard-wearing, easy to clean and good looking, it also feels warm and pleasant underfoot. Simply use the same wood as you have in other rooms, or opt for a lighter tone, to subtly zone the bedroom and gently set it apart from the more sociable rooms. Remember that you will probably walk on this floor barefoot, so if original boards are knotty or uneven, throw down rugs, sheepskins and hides to soften them and create some toe-tickling luxury.

You can afford to ease off the rustic gas when it comes to bedroom walls, too. Feature walls of brick, slate or reclaimed timber may feel a bit too cave-like for a sleeping space, so instead play around with paint colours for a lush, interesting effect without the masonry.

OPPOSITE Natural lime paint, which produces a soft, slightly uneven finish, has been applied halfway up this bedroom wall to create a dramatic border. A blanket in a similar, moody grey and a dark upholstered headboard beautifully complement this shade.

ABOVE Assorted cushion covers and pillowcases made from printed sacking are scattered across this bed, lending lots of texture and pattern. Adding a simply upholstered headboard in a muted tone to a divan/box spring bed helps it to look elegant and finished.

A soft, dove grey can be firmed up by alcoves painted in slate or plum. Pigmented plaster or an organic treatment such as lime paint also work well in a bedroom. They produce a slightly uneven, textured look that will add interest without overpowering this restful space. Use them to mark out a 'headboard' on the wall behind the bed, or apply all the way around the room just to waist height to create a border.

The bed is the largest and most important piece of furniture in a bedroom. It must look attractive, fit the scheme and also be a really comfortable place to sleep. We spend, on average, a third of our lifetime asleep, so it is worth investing in a quality mattress. Think about the style of bed that will fit the space, too. If you fancy a bedstead, from a modern four-poster to a classic sleigh bed, remember

ABOVE The owners of this Norwegian home have rejected the traditional Scandinavian scheme of white walls and floors punctuated by black and grey details. Instead, they have opted for a fiercely modern rustic look, with wooden panelling covering the walls in every bedroom. In this sleeping space, rustic cladding creates a cosy cabin feel.

OPPOSITE & RIGHT This light, bright Dutch apartment is situated in the eaves of the building and boasts huge wooden beams and big windows. The masculine feel of the architecture is softened by the addition of more playful, rustic touches, such as the branches hung with pictures, a lampshade that looks like silver birch bark and even a fluffy bunny!

THIS PAGE & OPPOSITE This bed canopy is made from reclaimed larch, also used to clad the living room walls and kitchen cabinets in this house. Here, it is installed horizontally to match the width of the bed. The twin chandeliers add a touch of glamour that works nicely against the rough timber. Patterned bedding in lush, jewel colours further softens the rustic feel, and vintage finds, from pictures to the bedside tables, bring pleasing detail. Again, as downstairs, a neutral oak floor creates the perfect backdrop to the grittier elements of this room.

ABOVE The deep, retro oranges on the bedding and curtains/drapes tie in beautifully with the dark, honey tones of the wooden headboard.
ABOVE RIGHT The pretty pattern of branches and fruit across these wardrobe/closet doors was designed by the home owner. It was cut from wood and glued to a milky Perspex, then incorporated into the doors.

RIGHT Mirrored tiles were originally fitted along the wall in this bedroom, but when the owner pulled them off, the glue that had fixed them in place left marks behind. She left these splotches and swirls, enjoying the unusual pattern they produce across the wall.

RIGHT Soft paint shades, which are reminiscent of sea and sky, give this bedroom a calm atmosphere. Pale grey walls are punctuated by an alcove in deep brown. This ties in with some of the antique furniture in the room, made from deep, dark wood. On top of the pure white bed linen, a single cushion brings a splash of colour and pattern to this neutral scheme.

BELOW Wardrobes/closets are often fitted into bedroom alcoves, but in this one display, rather than storage, is the priority. A simple wooden shelf is home to a vintage mirror and flowers, while a rustic stool makes a neat bedside table.

that darker frames tend to dominate a room and this can make it appear much smaller, whereas paler, less obtrusive frames will give the impression of light and space.

Upholstered beds are smart and stylish, creating a focal point in a room as well as introducing colour and softness – welcome in a modern rustic scheme. Upholstered beds have headboards integral to the main frame, while a traditional divan/box spring consists only of a deep timber-frame base with a solid or sprung top. Divans/box springs can be hollow, with storage underneath, or can have visible legs. It's always a good idea to team them with a wooden or upholstered headboard, otherwise they can look unfinished.

Now for the bedding. Stay loyal to the simple, natural palette that works so well in the other rooms of a modern rustic home. Plain white bed linen is a can't-fail option, its clean, fresh feel working as a great foil to any rugged features or wooden surfaces. Alternatively, choose sheets and duvet covers in soft oatmeal shades or deep, sexy greys. Invest in natural, breathable fabrics, which will bring pleasing weight and texture to your bed. Cotton with a high thread count (good-quality sheets start

LEFT A photo of one of the home owner's grandfathers has been enlarged and made into a gorgeous black and white wall covering in this bedroom (seen opposite).

BELOW LEFT & BELOW A combination of desk space, storage and open floor space are an asset in this child's room. Illustrations from a Dutch children's book have been blown up and papered to the wall behind the work area.

ABOVE & OPPOSITE

When the owners of this Dutch home converted it from barns and farm buildings, they used every scrap of original wood in new and exciting places. Here, painted floorboards from downstairs have been recycled upstairs to make a cosy child's cabin bed. It is a perfect hangout for a little boy and makes great use of space beneath the pitched roof. Hooks on the exterior provide handy storage.

RIGHT This boy's room has the same ply-covered walls as the other children's bedrooms in this house, but the addition of darker bedding and a cushion decorated with the American flag lend it a masculine edge. The modernist wall lamp provides directional reading light and looks striking.

at 180) is beautifully soft and smooth, while linen, woven from flax fibres, is durable, eco-friendly and anti-allergic.

A double bed occupies a large surface area, so once you have made it with your choice of bed linen, ratchet up its sensual appeal by layering on blankets, bedspreads and throws in a variety of materials. Blankets can be close and felted, or beautifully knitted with cable patterns or thick, chunky stitches. Add tactile softness with finer throws in anything from cashmere to brushed alpaca, too, or even throw over a sheepskin or hide, for a touch of cabin cosiness. Stick to muted colours, but don't rule out pattern. A pinstripe, plaid or embroidered fabric, in knocked-back tones or soft jewel shades, adds beguiling detail and depth.

The modern rustic look is earthy and bold, but in terms of furniture and decoration, it's actually rather minimal.

ABOVE LEFT Inexpensive ply has been used to line the walls in this bedroom, and to make the neat, streamlined furniture in here, for a fully co-ordinated and fresh, rustic feel.

LEFT Small cubby holes and box-shaped shelves have been built into this ply wall for the children to play with, display favourite toys in and even sit and read in.

RIGHT In this boy's room, a long table is positioned against one wall as a space for homework, craft projects or for displaying favourite pieces. The industrial-style stool has a height-adjustable swivel seat – perfect for a growing child!

BELOW RIGHT This custom-built child's bed is designed to look like a castle, complete with battlements, and incorporates a bed, play space and hooks for storage. The walls are kept bare, but a bright duvet adds a splash of colour and pattern.

Remember this as you design your bedroom and keep the space uncluttered. A wardrobe/closet and chest of drawers/dresser are essential clothes storage, but even the most beautiful armoire will take up a lot of space and can dominate a room, so consider having something built in. Alcoves and awkward corners that might otherwise have no role can be pressed into service, leaving the room clear for perhaps just one really beautiful piece.

When choosing freestanding furniture, opt for timeless styles with rugged integrity. Antique family heirlooms, such as a chest of drawers/dresser in rich mahogany, will fit in, and so, too, will something more classic: a mid-century modern occasional chair, perhaps, or a slender sideboard. Think carefully about size and scale before you buy. Any piece that does not provide storage should be kept on the small side, so shop around for the right item. Don't automatically choose a large bedside unit, for example, when a milking stool or simple, rustic shelf could do the job just as nicely, and take up less room.

As we have seen elsewhere, a modern rustic home does not brim with knick-knacks and 'objets', but that does not mean it is devoid of detail. Walls can take a little decoration, but choose discreet, softly-coloured artworks that will not fight with their background. Mirrors also work well in a bedroom. Hang something with a dark wooden or scuffed gilt frame for extra rustic style. A large mirror will

give you somewhere to check your appearance, too, so position it where you can easily see into it. It will also boost brightness levels, helpfully bouncing light around the space. Look out for vintage mirrors with silvered or misted glass, which will function as an artwork rather than a conventional looking glass.

Think less is more when it comes to displays. A few treasured pieces, arranged on a bedside table/nightstand or shelf, will add personality and round out the space, but to ensure the atmosphere remains restful, stick to small collections in harmonious colours and shapes. Don't overlook the decorative potential of the items that naturally belong in a bedroom. Jewellery can be hung from hooks to create a low-key display that also allows you to see all your pieces at a glance. You might also heap brooches or bangles into a beautiful stone platter or wooden bowl, and then keep essential but unattractive bottles, pots and jars in a lidded wooden box or a pretty mirrored cabinet.

Remember the impact of house plants and fresh flowers, too. A small potted fern or just a few hedgerow sprigs can create a pocket of natural beauty that will calm the senses and put you at your ease.

THIS PAGE Concrete brings a modern rustic feel to even the smallest bathroom. Here, a concrete sink, shelves and shower have been made bespoke to fit the space, and are then sealed and polished for durability and a smooth finish.

LEFT & FAR LEFT A rustic wooden bench, textured stone floor tiles and linen towels soften the slightly austere feel of a concrete bathroom. A vintage carved wooden peg rail provides hanging space, while old letters from a printing press mark the owner's initials above their towel.

BELOW Concrete has been used to make a stand here. A stone sink is mounted on top and a simple wooden shelf installed below, providing space for bathroom essentials. Baskets are a practical storage option and bring some rustic texture to the smooth sink surround.

BATHROOMS

A watery relaxation zone and somewhere for a quick wash and brush-up, today's bathrooms are hard-working, multi-tasking spaces that have both a practical and a pleasurable function. For that reason, they need careful planning, with a functional configuration, flexible lighting and ample storage factored in. We may want to build in the latest high-tech shower or a show-stopper bathtub, too, and the space must be beautifully finished so that we will linger here, when time allows. Natural materials, a favourite of all modern rustic homes, have long been used in bathrooms, from luxurious marble to simple slate flooring, but in today's modern rustic bathrooms, exciting treatments and finishes more commonly seen in entertaining spaces, including wood-effect tiles and polished concrete, are beautifully incorporated, giving this space unique personality.

BELOW This bathroom employs dark woods and finishes to create a cocooning, enveloping atmosphere. Black stained wood has been used to make a sleek sink stand, with drawers for storage beneath and a bright white sink on top as a punchy contrast.

RIGHT A dark stone sink and black taps/faucets are installed against a graphic backdrop of patterned tiles. The same dark palette of browns and blacks is used in this downstairs bathroom as in the larger bathroom, pictured opposite and below.

Building a bathroom can be as simple as installing a white suite and adding detail and colour. In a modern rustic scheme, the simple white suite is still a great foundation, but rather than choosing pieces that ape Edwardian bathroom design, for example, create a modern vibe with soft, contemporary shapes. Elegant trough-style sinks provide generous space and timeless good looks. Freestanding bathtubs are a beautiful take on the old-fashioned cast-iron tub, and some also replace the traditional claw feet with a chunky wooden base.

If space and budget allow, ditch the familiar, shop-bought bathtub, sink and toilet combo and look out for sanitary ware made from other interesting materials. Bathtubs made from wood (try William Garvey), copper and marble are available. Beautifully shaped oval bathtubs, made from lightweight composite material that looks like stone, are another stylish option and come in a range of shades. Admittedly, these gorgeous bathtubs are not cheap, but a big-ticket centrepiece can be flanked by inexpensive, high-street pieces and still look fabulous.

OPPOSITE When fitted into a dark wood surround, with a step leading up, a simple white tub becomes a luxurious bathing spot. Wooden walls add an intimate, sauna-like feel.

ABOVE LEFT A large trough sink with two taps/faucets provides plenty of space for the family to wash faces or brush teeth at the same time. Concrete has been used as a sink stand and bathtub surround, but the stone, wood and woven baskets mixed in keep the look the rustic side of minimal.

ABOVE RIGHT A walk-in shower has been fitted into the small amount of full-height space in this top-floor bathroom, nestled in the sloping eaves. The adjoining wall is the perfect space for a tall ladder-style towel rail, too, while a simple wooden stool is home to the soap.

Another stylish approach is to install an inexpensive bathtub or sink in a modern rustic surround. Flanking a run-of-the-mill tub in wood panelling or treating the walls around the bathtub sink and shower with waterproof tadelakt or concrete in a moody shade will mask their humble origins and bring rich, rustic style to the room. Similarly, set a simple white sink on a handsome, rustic stand fashioned from a farmhouse table or slab of reclaimed timber. Make sure you treat the wood with a waterproof sealant first, though, to protect it from splashes and spills.

Think about incorporating recycled sanitary ware, too. Many salvage yards sell sinks and handsome freestanding bathtubs already reconditioned and re-enamelled. For a super-rustic feel, look out for a piece that can be converted for bathroom service. An old cattle trough, butler's sink or even a solid piece of stone that could be carved and polished can all make striking additions to a modern rustic bathroom.

Well-planned lighting is essential in this much-used room. Build in plenty of ambient light as background illumination and ideally fit the lights on separate circuits so that you can have just a few on during a quiet evening soak. If that is not possible, install a simple dimmer switch instead to help you control the mood.

FAR RIGHT Fitting a bespoke concrete sink into this downstairs cloakroom makes good use of the limited space. The mirror adds a blast of rustic style.

RIGHT & BELOW A simple shelf unit topped with chunky reclaimed timber is the rustic base for a unique sink, carved from a single piece of stone. The sleek bathtub and the fireplace, fitted into the wall and also seen from the bedroom on the other side, are luxe modern touches.

BELOW A classic freestanding bathtub is the centrepiece here, with a rustic decoration hanging on the wall. These sticks were used to cultivate oysters, which would have grown on them, leaving a pale mark behind once picked off.

RIGHT This sleek, neat cloakroom has a whiff of modern rustic style thanks to the smooth birch veneer on the walls.

BELOW RIGHT A piece of found timber, varnished to make it splash resistant, forms a stand for this simple sink.

LEFT & RIGHT Fitting a sink across an alcove cleverly uses otherwise redundant space in this shower room.
BELOW RIGHT This low partition wall hides the toilet behind and incorporates plumbing for the bathtub.

When planning the position and quantity of lights, remember that any dark notes and matt surfaces will swallow light, so avoid fitting a single central pendant and try to work in several different sources, spread out over the room. Low-voltage recessed LED downlights are a great option, and should be used above bath and shower areas in any case, as they are safe in these damp zones. Wall lights fitted either side of a mirror are also useful, providing good illumination for shaving or applying make-up.

With the sanitary ware and surfaces in place, enjoy completing the space with some modern rustic styling. Tracking down complementary pieces is easy. Everything from shelves to soap dishes and storage boxes are available in wood. Similarly, baskets woven from natural materials will fit in beautifully and can be used for laundry, towels or bottles. Consider the practical as well as the decorative. A knotty bamboo ladder will add height to your scheme, but can also be used to hang towels on.

Finally, sprinkle over a few more decorative additions, to subtly personalize the space. Seashells piled into glass jars; a bunch of fresh flowers in an earthenware jug/pitcher; a beautiful linen towel with a pretty fringe or an attractive soap dish – they will all do much to soften, but not dilute, the modern rustic feel.

ABOVE The floor tiles were originally in the living quarters of this renovated Dutch farm building. The round opening in the wall use to be a hole with a cover for ventilation, but now the addition of stained glass has turned it into a feature.

RIGHT & FAR RIGHT The wide brick-built sink is sealed in waterproof concrete with state-of-the-art taps/faucets above.

THIS PAGE A waterproof plaster finish with a green-grey tint has been used on the floor and walls in this spacious bathroom. Light floods in from the Velux windows above, leaving the wall space clear for a large towel ladder, propped against it. It was made by the owner and her children, using tree branches secured with coloured ribbon.

RIGHT & FAR RIGHT
Favourite photographs
and images cover the
noticeboard in this work
space, while a small
shelf is home to a few
essentials, including
a lamp and a radio.
BELOW Sewing supplies
and materials are neatly
stored in card boxes on
this shelf unit.

OPPOSITE A noticeboard,
hanging above the desk
of the fashion designer
and potter who owns this
house, acts as a giant
mood board, crowded
with inspiration. A high
work bench is dotted
with homemade pots
and a nearby window
provides natural light
to work by.

WORK SPACES

The modern home office is a multi-
tasker – a place where practicality,
productive design and personal style
meet. Of course, we don't all have a dedicated
office – or even need one – but a desk where
you can sort paperwork, work on craft projects or
tackle homework is still a much-valued addition.
In a largely open-plan home, slot a desk that tones
in with your furniture along one wall or simply
make the most of an unused corner. Space at the
end of a hallway, under the stairs or on a landing
can become a quiet working zone. If the area is
visible from other rooms, keep it tidy. A cluttered
desk is the enemy of productivity and, after hours,
is an unwelcome distraction, reminding you of
unfinished tasks.

Whether your work space is part of a room or entirely separate, it still needs to feel unique and uplifting. So forget standard office furniture and kit it out with pieces that reflect your personality. There are plenty of options that combine modern rustic style with simple functionality. You may find a beautiful antique desk – a mid-century piece, perhaps – that perfectly suits your scheme, or consider using a long dining table or simple kitchen prep table, too. Always check that you can sit at your proposed desk comfortably, with the worktop neither squashing your legs nor awkwardly high. If you have plenty of space, construct your own desk by supporting a plain length of timber with plan chests or low filing cabinets.

Your office space will need some storage to function well. Built-in storage is a good option. Tall cupboards take up relatively little floor space, but conceal a wealth of paperwork and work paraphernalia. Scour vintage markets for wire

LEFT & OPPOSITE This work station, made from trestle legs topped with a found piece of imitation concrete, has been squeezed into a corner of a bedroom. A few decorative pieces keep the space inspiring.
ABOVE RIGHT & RIGHT A tall, industrial wooden work bench looks at home in this modern barn. It has handy storage space, where drawers were perhaps once fitted, and simple stools provide flexible seating. Propped along the wall, the striking Shipwreck prints are by Leah Fusco.

baskets, wooden crates and trays that can hold anything from files to staplers and sticky notes. Metal filing cabinets are the original office storage, but their painted finishes can look rather dreary. Consider sanding and repainting one, or find a salvage yard or vintage store which stocks them already stripped and sandblasted. This treatment produces a soft, gleaming metal finish that is light years away from the dull greens and greys these office workhorses typically come in.

No work space is complete without a chair, but do not assume you have to choose something serious and officey. If you like the classic swivel chair style, that's fine, but why not track down a vintage version in leather and aluminium? If you are unlikely to be sitting at your desk for long stretches and ergonomics are less of a consideration, you can throw the search wider and choose anything from a bench to a design classic chair. Vintage markets are great sources of interesting seating, often very reasonably priced. Stools with

metal legs and wooden seats often crop up and make handy additional seating that can be stacked and stored when not in use. Remember to take along your desk measurements when chair shopping, and check that the seat is the right height to fit under your work station before you buy.

Make sure your lighting supports your work, too. Wall lights will provide a good wash of ambient light, but a task light, positioned on the desk, will help you with close work such as reading or sewing. Either a classic anglepoise or a Jieldé lamp are both a perfect fit in a modern rustic office, combining iconic good looks with helpful, directional light. Find an original on eBay or in a second-hand shop.

With the practicalities in place, you can enjoy dotting your space with inspiring objects. Obviously, clutter will not boost your productivity, but a few treasured modern rustic pieces, from a much-loved painting to a jug of flowers, will enhance your mood, helping you to work more efficiently.

OUTSIDE SPACE

Whether you have acres of land or a neat city balcony, injecting your outside space with some modern rustic style is easy. Forget planting plans and landscaping, for most of us creating a sociable, functional area for alfresco lunches or afternoon snoozing is more about employing ideas used inside than full-on garden design. Think of your outdoor area as an exterior room, which can be styled in exactly the same way as the rooms within the house. Choose furniture that is in keeping with pieces inside, or simply borrow items normally at home in the living room or kitchen for occasional use outside. Stick to the same colours, textiles and even materials that give the interior its modern rustic personality, for a beautifully cohesive look that links outside and in.

OPPOSITE A small courtyard, dotted with potted plants and a Buddha head, stands between the bedroom and bathroom, giving a green view from both spaces.

RIGHT & BELOW Potted plants are a key feature of this LA home. Inside, they help add some organic colour to the brick and stone that the house is made from. They also feature outside on a mirrored shelf made from an old, found cabinet, installed by the front door. The plants sit in pots designed and thrown by the owner. A branch makes a natural sculpture.

Modern rustic style translates effortlessly to any outside space, whether it is a shady city courtyard or a spacious rural garden. This look champions the use of natural materials, so it is a perfect fit outdoors, and the woody tones and lush greens of even the most modest garden will inform the furniture, finishes and details you use.

As the outside space is often visible through windows or glass doors, it is important to create a feeling of the inside and outside merging. The outside space should not be a separate zone, tacked onto the house, but a seamless extension of the interior. Adopt the same style outside as in, even employing the same raw materials and finishes here. Timber cladding, concrete flooring or textured plaster can be used outside, to link the two areas, and any accent colours dotted through your home can be used outside, too.

Seating is crucial in any outside space, and a mix of built-in and freestanding pieces works well. A long bench built against a house or boundary wall makes good use of space and may incorporate storage below, for folding chairs or tools. Just make sure it is watertight if you plan to keep seat pads and cushions in it.

Elsewhere, choose plastic chairs with metal legs, reminiscent of those found in schools, as

LEFT & RIGHT Thanks to its hillside position, this house and its terrace have long views. The dark wooden seating and table are clashed with yellow cushions, while a patterned rug adds detail. A fire pit makes the space usable year round.

a fun contrast to a rustic table, or source vintage garden furniture such as café chairs and folding metal tables. For a more pop feel, invest in a single, striking lounger from a contemporary designer. Then simply add kit from indoors. Cutlery/flatware, baskets, throws and cushions used indoors will work outside, and can simply be brought in at night.

The planting in a modern rustic outside space is reminiscent of wild, woodland areas, with neither the abundant flowers of a cottage garden nor the sharp lines of a designed, urban exterior. Think ferns, low bushes, informal hedges and trees. They bring masses of green while masking unsightly boundary walls and also offer privacy.

Potted plants are invaluable and can be moved around to help zone areas or soften the hard lines of a terrace or fence. Where room is tight, pots can take up valuable floor space, so build in shelves for them or grow hanging or climbing plants. Finally, dress your table with small plants potted in zinc or ceramic containers – they look great and, unlike cut flowers, will last, too.

LEFT Old school chairs in vibrant yellow plastic flank a simple table, their colour popping out against the dark green shrubs and unpaved ground. Potted plants make a lush centrepiece.

OPPOSITE On the front porch, just inside the gate, a built-in bench is teamed with a simple wood and metal table, and brightened up with a pink cushion pad and colourful tableware.

PICTURE CREDITS

Endpapers The family home of Clare Checkland and Ian Harding in Fife; 1 The home of Erica Farjo and David Slade; 2 www.stylexclusief.nl; 3 The cabin of Hanne Borge and her family in Norway; 4–5 The family home of Gina Portman of Folk at Home www.folkathome.com; 6 The family home of the interior designer Larissa van Seumeren in the Netherlands; 7 left The home of Jonathan Sela and Megan Schoenbachler; 7 right The cabin of Hanne Borge and her family in Norway; 8–9 Oliver Heath and Katie Weiner – sustainable architecture, interior and jewellery design; 10–11 The family home of Gina Portman of Folk at Home www.folkathome.com; 12–13 www.stylexclusief.nl; 14–15 The family home of Johan Gjendem and Vibeke Rognan in Oslo, designed by architect Knut Hjeltnes; 16–17 The family home of Clare Checkland and Ian Harding in Fife; 18–19 Barbara Bestor, www.bestorarchitecture.com; 20–23 Oliver Heath and Katie Weiner – sustainable architecture, interior and jewellery design; 24–25 The family home of the interior designer Larissa van Seumeren in the Netherlands; 26–27 The home of interior stylist and ceramic designer Silje Aune Eriksen of thisis-blog.blogspot.com; 28–29 The cabin of Hanne Borge and her family in Norway; 30 below left The home of Erica Farjo and David Slade; 30–33 Barbara Bestor, www.bestorarchitecture.com; 34–35 The home of Erica Farjo and David Slade; 36 below Barbara Bestor, www.bestorarchitecture.com; 36 above–37 The home of interior stylist and ceramic designer Silje Aune Eriksen of thisis-blog.blogspot.com; 38–41 The Los Angeles home of Adam and Kate Blackman, www.blackmancruz.com; 42–43 Tracy Wilkinson www.twworkshop.com; 44–45 The home of Matthew and Gillian Chessé; 46–47 The cabin of Hanne Borge and her family in Norway; 48 The family home of the interior designer Larissa van Seumeren in the Netherlands; 49 above left The home of Jonathan Sela and Megan Schoenbachler; 49 above right The cabin of Hanne Borge and her family in Norway; 49 below right Oliver Heath and Katie Weiner–sustainable architecture, interior and jewellery design; 49 below right The cabin of Hanne Borge and her family in Norway; 50–51 The home of Jonathan Sela and Megan Schoenbachler; 52 Tracy Wilkinson www.twworkshop.com; 53 left The family home of the interior designer Larissa van Seumeren in the Netherlands; 53 centre The family home of Johan Gjendem and Vibeke Rognan in Oslo, designed by architect Knut Hjeltnes; 53 right Tracy Wilkinson www.twworkshop.com; 54 above left The home of Jonathan Sela and Megan Schoenbachler; 54 above & below right The family home of Gina Portman of Folk at Home www.folkathome.com; 54 below left Oliver Heath and Katie Weiner – sustainable architecture, interior and jewellery design; 55 The family home of Clare Checkland and Ian Harding in Fife; 56 The cabin of Hanne Borge and her family in Norway; 57 above left The family home of Gina Portman of Folk at Home www.folkathome.com; 57 above centre The cabin of Hanne Borge and her family in Norway; 57 above right The Los Angeles home of Adam and Kate Blackman, www.blackmancruz.com; 57 below left and centre www.stylexclusief.nl; 57 below right The home of interior stylist and ceramic designer Silje Aune Eriksen of thisis-blog.blogspot.com; 58 The cabin of Hanne Borge and her family in Norway; 59 The family home of the interior designer Larissa van Seumeren in the Netherlands; 60 The Los Angeles home of Adam and Kate Blackman, www.blackmancruz.com; 61 above and below left The family home of Johan Gjendem and Vibeke Rognan in Oslo, designed by architect Knut Hjeltnes; 61 below right The Los Angeles home of Adam and Kate Blackman, www.blackmancruz.com; 62 above left Tracy Wilkinson www.twworkshop.com; 62 above centre Barbara Bestor, www.bestorarchitecture.com; 62 above right The home of Erica Farjo and David Slade; 63 The home of Matthew and Gillian Chessé; 64 above left Oliver Heath and Katie Weiner – sustainable architecture, interior and jewellery design; 64 above right and below left The cabin of Hanne Borge and her family in Norway; 64 below right The family home of Johan Gjendem and Vibeke Rognan in Oslo, designed by architect Knut Hjeltnes; 65 The cabin of Hanne Borge and her family in Norway; 66 above left Tracy Wilkinson www.twworkshop.com; 66 above right The family home of Johan Gjendem and Vibeke Rognan in Oslo, designed by architect Knut Hjeltnes; 66 below left The family home of Clare Checkland and Ian Harding in Fife; 67 The home of Erica Farjo and David Slade; 68 The cabin of Hanne Borge and her family in Norway; 69 above left The home of interior stylist and ceramic designer Silje Aune Eriksen of thisis-blog.blogspot.com; 69 above right The family home of Johan Gjendem and Vibeke Rognan in Oslo, designed by architect Knut Hjeltnes; 69 below left The home of interior stylist and ceramic designer Silje Aune Eriksen of thisis-blog.blogspot.com; 69 below right The cabin of Hanne Borge and her family in Norway; 70 above left The home of Jonathan Sela and Megan Schoenbachler; 70 above right left The family home of Clare Checkland and Ian Harding in Fife; 70 below left Oliver Heath and Katie Weiner – sustainable architecture, interior and jewellery design; 71 The family home of the interior designer Larissa van Seumeren in the Netherlands; 72 above left The cabin of Hanne Borge and her family in Norway; 72 above and below right Oliver Heath and Katie Weiner – sustainable architecture, interior and jewellery design; 72 below left The cabin of Hanne Borge and her family in Norway; 73 Oliver Heath and Katie Weiner – sustainable architecture, interior and jewellery design; 74 The home of Jonathan Sela and Megan Schoenbachler; 75 The Los Angeles home of Adam and Kate Blackman, www.blackmancruz.com; 76–77 The cabin of Hanne Borge and her family in Norway; 78–79 www.stylexclusief.nl; 80–81 The family home of the interior designer Larissa van Seumeren in the Netherlands; 82–83 The home of Jonathan Sela and Megan Schoenbachler; 84–85 Tracy Wilkinson www.twworkshop.com; 86 Oliver Heath and Katie Weiner – sustainable architecture, interior and jewellery design; 87 The home of interior stylist and ceramic designer Silje Aune Eriksen of thisis-blog.blogspot.com; 88–91 The cabin of Hanne Borge and her family in Norway; 92–93 The family home of Gina Portman of Folk at Home www.folkathome.com; 94–95 right The family home of Johan Gjendem and Vibeke Rognan in Oslo, designed by architect Knut Hjeltnes; 96–97 www.stylexclusief.nl; 98–101 The cabin of Hanne Borge and her family in Norway; 102–103 The family home of Clare Checkland and Ian Harding in Fife; 104–105 The family home of Johan Gjendem and Vibeke Rognan in Oslo, designed by architect Knut Hjeltnes; 106–107 Oliver Heath and Katie Weiner – sustainable architecture, interior and jewellery design; 108–109 The family home of Gina Portman of Folk at Home www.folkathome.com; 110–111 The family home of the interior designer Larissa van Seumeren in the Netherlands; 112–113 The home of Jonathan Sela and Megan Schoenbachler; 114 The Los Angeles home of Adam and Kate Blackman, www.blackmancruz.com; 115 Tracy Wilkinson www.twworkshop.com; 116–117 The Los Angeles home of Adam and Kate Blackman, www.blackmancruz.com; 118 The family home of Gina Portman of Folk at Home www.folkathome.com; 119 www.stylexclusief.nl; 120 left The family home of Johan Gjendem and Vibeke Rognan in Oslo, designed by architect Knut Hjeltnes; 120 right–121 The home of interior stylist and ceramic designer Silje Aune Eriksen of thisis-blog.blogspot.com; 122–123 Oliver Heath and Katie Weiner – sustainable architecture, interior and jewellery design; 124 left The home of Jonathan Sela and Megan Schoenbachler; 124 above right The home of Matthew and Gillian Chessé; 124 below right Tracy Wilkinson www.twworkshop.com; 125 The family home of Clare Checkland and Ian Harding in Fife; 126–127 The family home of the interior designer Larissa van Seumeren in the Netherlands; 128 The family home of Johan Gjendem and Vibeke Rognan in Oslo, designed by architect Knut Hjeltnes; 129 above The family home of Gina Portman of Folk at Home www.folkathome.com; 129 below The home of Jonathan Sela and Megan Schoenbachler; 130–133 The cabin of Hanne Borge and her family in Norway; 134–135 The home of Jonathan Sela and Megan Schoenbachler; 136–137 www.stylexclusief.nl; 138 The family home of Clare Checkland and Ian Harding in Fife; 139 The family home of Gina Portman of Folk at Home www.folkathome.com; 140–141 The family home of the interior designer Larissa van Seumeren in the Netherlands; 142–143 Tracy Wilkinson www.twworkshop.com; 144–145 left The home of interior stylist and ceramic designer Silje Aune Eriksen of thisis-blog.blogspot.com; 145 right The family home of Gina Portman of Folk at Home www.folkathome.com; 146 The family home of the interior designer Larissa van Seumeren in the Netherlands; 147 The family home of Johan Gjendem and Vibeke Rognan in Oslo, designed by architect Knut Hjeltnes; 148–150 The home of Jonathan Sela and Megan Schoenbachler; 151 Tracy Wilkinson www.twworkshop.com; 152–153 Barbara Bestor, www.bestorarchitecture.com; 160 left www.stylexclusief.nl; 160 centre Tracy Wilkinson www.twworkshop.com; 160 right The home of Erica Farjo and David Slade.

CREDITS

ADAM AND KATE BLACKMAN
BLACKMAN CRUZ
836 North Highland Avenue
Los Angeles
CA 90038
T: +1 323 466 8600
www.blackman.cruz
and
ARCHITECT: A. QUINCY JONES FAIA
(1913–1979)
38–41, 57 above right, 60,
61 below right, 75, 114,
116–117.

BARBARA BESTOR,
BARBARA BESTOR ARCHITECTURE
3920 Fountain Avenue
Los Angeles
CA 90029
T: +1 323 666 9399
www.bestorarchitecture.com
1, 18–19, 30 below left,
30–33, 34–35, 36 below, 62
above centre,62 above right,
67, 152–153, 160 right.

OLIVER CHAPMAN ARCHITECTS
36 St Mary's Street
Edinburgh
EH1 1SX
T: +44 (0)131 477 4513
E: admin@oliverchapman
architects.com
www.oliverchapmanarchitects.
com
Endpapers, 16–17, 55, 66
below left, 70 above right,
102–103, 125, 138.

Flowers and closet doors
designed and crafted by the
owner Gillian Chessé
44–45, 63, 124 above right.

GINA PORTMAN
www.folkathome.com
and
Shipwreck Prints by Leah Fusco
www.leahfusco.co.uk
4–5, 10–11, 54 above, 54
below right, 57 above left,
92–93, 108–109, 118, 129
above, 139, 145 right.

HANNE BORGE
BOLINA
E: netshop@bolina.no
T: +47 67 53 61 45
www.bolina.no
3, 7 right, 28–29, 46–47, 49
above right, 49 below right, 56,
57 above centre, 58, 64 above
right, 64 below left, 65, 68, 69
below right, 72 above left, 72
below left, 76–77, 88–91,
98–101, 130–133.

KNUT HJELTNES AS
SIVILARKITEKTER
Professor Dahlsgate 16
0355 Oslo
Norway
T: +47 22 69 17 35
E: knut@hjeltnes.as
www.hjeltnes.as
14–15, 53 centre, 61 above,
61 below left, 64 below left, 66
above right, 69 above right, 94,
95 right, 104–105, 120 left,
128, 147.

VIVA VIDA B.V.
INTERIOR DESIGN STUDIO
Rijksstraatweg 26
3545 NA Utrecht
The Netherlands
and
STUDIO: BEEFLAND 1
3454JD De Meern
The Netherlands
E info@vivavida.nl
www.vivavida.nl
6, 24–25, 48, 53 left, 59, 71,
80–81, 110–111, 126–127,
140–141, 146.

MEGAN SCHOENBACHLER
PHOTOGRAPHY
www.meganschoenbachler.com
and
ARCHITECTS:
MARMOL RADZINER ARCHITECTURE
12210 Nebraska Avenue
Los Angeles
CA 90025
T: +1 310 826 6222
www.marmol-radziner.com
7 left, 49 above left, 50–51,
54 above left, 70 above left, 74,
82–83,112–113, 124 left, 129
below, 134–135, 148–150.

OLIVER HEATH
www.oliverheath.com
and
KATIE WEINER
www.katieweiner.com
8–9, 20–23, 49 below right,
54 below left, 64 above left, 70
below left, 72 above, 72 below
right, 73, 86, 106–107,
122–123.

SILJE AUNE ERIKSEN
thisis-blog.blogspot.com
E: thisismailforyou@gmail.com
28–29, 36 above, 37, 57 below
right, 69 above right, 69 below
left, 87, 120 right, 121, 144,
145 left.

TRACY WILKINSON
www.twworkshop.com
42–43, 52, 53 right, 62 above
left, 66 above left, 84, 85, 115,
124 below right, 142–143,
151, 160 centre.

STYLEXCLUSIEF
Bospolderweg 5
2355 CG Hoogmade
The Netherlands
T: +31 (0)23 2302723
Email: info@stylexclusief.nl
www.stylexclusief.nl
Opening days: Tuesday,
Thursday and Friday or you
can visit us by appointment
on other days
2, 12–13, 57 below left, 57
centre, 78–79, 96–97, 119,
136–137, 160 left.

SOURCES

USA

ANTHROPOLOGIE
www.anthropologie.com
Stores all over the US and now in the UK. Furniture, textiles, and unusual bits and pieces for the bohemian rustic home. New and one-off vintage furniture. Inspiring display and merchandising throughout their stores (remember, that's how I got my start in this business!)

BROOK FARM GENERAL STORE
75 South 6th Street
Brooklyn, NY 11249
www.brookfarmgeneralstore.com
A small neighbourhood shop with a beautifully curated collection for every room in the home, including hammam towels, wool throws, and woven hampers. Good website and international shipping.

CRAIGSLIST
www.craigslist.org
I've bought and sold so many pieces of furniture via this site. You often find architectural salvage on there as well.

HERRIOTT GRACE
www.herriottgrace.com
Canadian father-daughter duo selling one-of-a-kind handmade items for the kitchen – think hand-turned wooden spoons, cake stands and beeswax candles.

MELROSE TRADING POST
7850 Melrose Avenue
Los Angeles, CA 90046
www.melrosetradingpost.org
Flea market held every Sunday at Fairfax High School. Laid back and small, this is not necessarily for serious antiques hunting but good for vintage art and smaller items.

MOHAWK GENERAL STORE
4011 W. Sunset Blvd
Los Angeles, CA 90029
www.mohawkgeneralstore.net
Mostly fashion on the website, but in store there are earthy-cool rustic home accessories and textiles.

POKETO
820 East 3rd Street
Los Angeles, CA 90013
www.poketo.com/poketo-store
Its plywood walls and splashes of colour make Poketo the perfect stop for your pop rustic needs.

ROSE BOWL FLEA MARKET
Pasadena, CA 91103
www.rgcshows.com
Second Sunday of every month. I used to live 5 minutes from here and I've both bought and sold at this legendary market.

SMALL ADVENTURE
www.smalladventureshop.com
Beautifully illustrated prints and paper goods inspired by nature and wildlife, by artist Keiko Brodeur. Perfect for a modern rustic kids rooms.

TW WORKSHOP
www.twworkshop.com
I fell in love with Tracy Wilkinson's handmade pottery and lighting when we shot her Los Angeles home.

WEST ELM
www.westelm.com
Online and all over the US. Good selection of clean-lined wooden tables, benches and storage baskets.

WORLD MARKET
www.worldmarket.com
Dotted all over the US, these stores stock a budget-friendly mix of rustic, industrial and ethnic furniture, textiles and homewares.

UK & EUROPE

ASTIER DE VILLATTE
www.astierdevillatte.com
Absolutely stunning handmade earthenware, glassware, and paper goods. Eye-wateringly pricey, but so beautiful and unique. Their cups and saucers showed up at many houses in this book. Cool website too.

BAILEYS HOME AND GARDEN
Whitecross Farm, Bridstow,
Ross-on-Wye, Herefordshire,
HR9 6JU
www.baileyshomeandgarden.com
Lighting, cookware, wooden toys, storage baskets – it's all here. And it's all simple, useful, well made and natural. Visit their sprawling shop set up in a group of farm buildings.

BLOOMINGVILLE
www.bloomingville.com
Danish brand stocking everything from tables and textiles to candles and lighting. Natural and earthy with pops of neon.

BODIE AND FOU
www.bodieandfou.com
Furniture, lighting and accessories including gorgeous linen duvet sets and cool modern accessories.

BOLINA
http://bolina.no
Hanne Borge's Norwegian store with new and vintage furniture and accessories. Expertly curated, pure, modern rustic pieces.

FOLKLORE
193 Upper Street
Islington
London N1 1RQ
www.shopfolklore.com
Lovely selection of simple, functional and natural home goods. Great lamps, cushions and throws. They also carry a selection of 'trompe-l'oeil' wallpapers that look like salvaged wood.

HAPPY PIECE
www.happypiece.com
Beautiful, brightly coloured hand-woven sisal baskets. Handmade by women in Rwanda, providing income and teaching valuable skills, and with profits going towards their education.

IKEA
www.ikea.com
So many great pieces for adding a modern edge to a rustic space. The key is to mix it with earthy-rustic and older pieces to avoid the showroom look. It's my go-to place for inexpensive sheepskin rugs and modern lighting. I'm an Ikea fan and I'm proud of it!

LABOUR AND WAIT
85 Redchurch Street
London E2 7DJ
www.labourandwait.co.uk
Well-designed, functional and timeless homewares – from rope doorstops to Welsh blankets.

LASSCO
www.lassco.co.uk
England's prime resource for architectural salvage. Not cheap, but some amazing stuff.

LIBERTY
Regent Street
London W1B 5AH
www.liberty.co.uk
Liberty's iconic building houses an eclectic and ever-changing collection of homewares. An excellent source for lighting, fabric and quirky accessories.

MADE BY YOLLY
http://yolandachiaramello.tumblr.com
My go-to florist for photo shoots, events and weddings, Yolly is also a brilliant photographer. She has an incredible eye and knows how to put together a stunning earthy and modern rustic look. (She's also the most stylish person I know.)

MERCI
111 boulevard Beaumarchais
75003 Paris
www.merci-merci.com
Three floors of food, fashion and home goods mixing high-end with new emerging artists. Has to be seen to be believed.

MINT
2 North Terrace
London SW3 2BA
www.mintshop.co.uk
A stunning collection of furniture and accessories from established and emerging designers. A lot of great pieces that use rustic elements in seriously modern ways.

RETROUVIUS
1016 Harrow Rd
London NW10 5NS
www.retrouvius.com
Ever-changing stock of architectural salvage, vintage furniture and unusual bits and pieces like old signage and medical posters.

SALVO
www.salvo.co.uk
If you're looking for reclaimed wood to give your home the modern rustic look, this is a great place to start. Lists of dealers of antique, salvage and reclaimed goods.

SEARCH & RESCUE
121 Stoke Newington Church Street
London N16 0UH
www.searchandrescueshop.co.uk
Forget the website, you must visit the newly re-designed shop itself for home accessories, lighting, one-off vintage pieces and giant floor cushions made in-house.

SKANDIUM
www.skandium.com
Stores in London and online offer the best in Scandinavian design in the UK. Clean lines, beautiful design, and an excellent resource for the pure and pop rustic looks. I love their lighting, stools and benches.

TOAST
www.toast.co.uk
Lovely selection of terracotta bowls, plates and mugs.

SUNBURY ANTIQUES MARKET AT KEMPTON PARK
www.sunburyantiques.com
Two Tuesdays a month. Opens at 6.30am. Most go very early to get the good stuff.

UNTO THIS LAST
230 Brick Lane
London E2 7EB
www.untothislast.co.uk
These guys make the coolest birch ply furniture in the back of their East London workshop, all on a digital router. You can't get more modern rustic than that! I love their chairs, wardrobes, and coat-stands.

For regular antiques fairs, check www.iacf.co.uk

INDEX

ACKNOWLEDGMENTS

I am so grateful to all at Ryland Peters & Small for giving me the opportunity to fulfil a dream. Thank you for seeing possibility in my idea and for working so hard to bring it to fruition: Cindy Richards, Leslie Harrington, Annabel Morgan, Megan Smith, Rebecca Woods and particularly Jess Walton, without whom I wouldn't have found such amazing locations (or stayed in such comfy hotels).

To Catherine Gratwicke, whose stunning photography captured the essence of Modern Rustic and whose friendship made the creation of this book such a pleasure. I couldn't have asked for a better travelling companion (and fellow foodie) as we jetted to Scotland, Los Angeles, Norway, the Netherlands and the UK.

A huge thanks to Joanna Simmons, whose gifted writing was far more eloquent than anything I could have come up with. You really got it. I want to thank all the wonderful homeowners who so graciously welcomed Cath and I with all our gear, fed us snacks, kept us caffeinated, and just let us get on with it.

Thanks to all those who have followed my blog over the years and showed such loyal support. It's what keeps me going. Your comments and feedback are very much appreciated.

Thanks, finally, to my amazing family who have supported me and believed in me over the years. My loving mum (who no doubt has already ordered 100 copies), my sister and brothers, all my in-laws. And of course my incredible husband and best friend Erick and our gorgeous children Johnny and Ella, who put up with so much all in the name of 'Mum's creative side'.